Borderline Personality Disorder: Looking for Symptoms in a Shortened Lifetime

Jimmy F. Kamada

Golden Eagle Publishing & Distributing

My Name Is Kathy And I Have BPD

Copyright © 2018 by Jimmy F. Kamada

All rights reserved. No part of this book can be reproduced, photocopied, transmitted or otherwise distributed in any printed or electronic form without written permission.

First Edition published by Golden Eagle Publishing & Distributing LLC, Moses Lake, WA 98837.

Printed by Create Space, an Amazon.com Company

ISBN-13: 978-0-692-07577-7
ISBN-10: 0692075771

Disclaimer: This book is a fictionalized account based on a combination of some real and some unsubstantiated events in Kathy's life as perceived by the author. The names of most of the individuals have been changed in this fictional work. Any resemblance to actual persons, living or dead is coincidental. All behaviors suggested by the author to be BPD symptoms are based entirely on the author's interpretations of the nine symptoms provided by the American Psychiatric Association's Diagnostic and Statistical Manual of Mental Disorder, Fourth Edition (DSM-IV) and is not intended as a medical diagnosis.

CONTENTS

1. Introduction   1
2. My Birth Parents   11
3. My Grade School Years   15
4. My Junior High School Years   23
5. My High School Years   25
6. My Childhood and Growing Up   27
7. My Young Adult Life   55
8. My First Marriage   65
9. My First House   83
10. My Second House   91
11. My Second Marriage   95
12. My Third House   97
13. Life's Challenges   103
14. A Christmas to Remember   107
15. Good Times Don't Last Forever   111
16. Going to Shelton and Starting New   113
17. Living in Redmond and My Third Marriage   127
18. My Mother Abandons Me   135
19. Insights into My Mind Through Greeting Cards   143
20. Life Alone and No Good Luck   147
    Notes   161
    References   161

MY NAME IS KATHY AND I HAVE BPD

Introduction

"My name is Kathy and I have BPD" is a fictionalized account based on some real and some unsubstantiated events in my daughter's life. Kathy speaks in the first person, but these are her thoughts as perceived and verbalized by her father and author. Kathy's own words are only those that are quoted in the letters, emails and cards within this book. To help the reader connect and understand, the actions, incidents, and thoughts in Kathy's life, there are bolded and italicized words in and at the end of paragraphs that reference back to the BPD symptoms, in the opinion of the author.

It is the hope of this book that someone will relate to BPD symptoms in a spouse, child, relative, friend, love interest or co-worker, and will try to learn more about Borderline Personality Disorder. There are more and more books being written about BPD. "Stop Walking on

Eggshells" by Paul T. Mason, MS and Randi Kreger is a must read[i]. If a psychiatric diagnosis of BPD is determined by a qualified professional, a referral to a long-term treatment plan can be pursued to help the BPD victim, provided there is a commitment by the victim and their support group.

What is BPD? It is Borderline Personality Disorder and it is defined as nine symptoms by the American Psychiatric Association's Diagnostic and Statistical Manual of Mental Disorder, Fourth Edition (DSM-IV). A diagnosis of BPD is established when five of the nine symptoms are observed. These nine symptoms are:

- **An intense fear of abandonment** – terrifying fear, real or imagined of being abandoned, left alone, separated or rejected

- **A pattern of intense relationships** – the extreme of falling quickly in love and quickly to bitter hatred

- **A distorted and unstable self-image** – feeling good about yourself and hating yourself, even perceiving yourself as evil

- **Impulsive, self-destructive behaviors** – engaging in impulse spending, binge eating, unsafe sex, gambling, drug and/or alcohol abuse

- **Suicidal and self-harming behaviors** – thinking about suicide, making suicide threats or attempting suicide or self-harming by cutting or burning

- **Extreme emotional swings** - unstable emotions or moods that are short-lived but swing from intense happiness to despondency, irritability, shame or anxiety over little things

- **Chronic feelings of emptiness** – uncomfortable feelings of a hole or void inside of them, feeling worthless, and not being satisfied

- **Inappropriate, intense or uncontrollable anger** – explosive anger and short temper directed outward or inward. Consumed by rage, sarcasm, bitterness or physical fights

- **Having severe dissociative symptoms** – feeling paranoia or suspicion of other's motives, losing touch with reality and under stressful situations may experience out of body feelings

Borderline Personality Disorder has only been officially recognized by mental health professionals since 1980. It is estimated that BPD affects 5.9% of adults at some time in their life according to the National Education Alliance for Borderline Personality Disorder. Full recovery from this disorder is possible with a long and intensive mental health treatment plan. There are different approaches to treating the symptoms of BPD. Some of the acute symptoms respond to treatment more effectively than others. There are cases where BPD symptoms are stabilized to the point that the affected person can demonstrate significant improvement over time, and not be observed as having five of the nine symptoms. However, a trigger could re-ignite the presence of one or more of the symptoms at any point in time.

Whatever psychotherapy is considered, it is critical to have a commitment from the BPD patient to want to change. As it is with alcohol or drug addiction, the road to recovery begins with the desire to change and the commitment to reinforce daily the thoughts and actions to fight off regressive behaviors. It is a daily struggle of extreme challenges and immense rewards that must be positively reinforced by the non-addicted.

Is the cause of Borderline Personality Disorder the function of *nature or nurture?* Many in the scientific and mental health communities feel that there is a greater possibility of developing BPD based on genetics and environmental influences, including harmful childhood experiences. No conclusive cause-and-effect relationship has been established.

Is there a cure for Borderline Personality Disorder? There is no easy treatment plan, quick fix or combination of medications that can transform someone with BPD into a non-BPD. There are many types of psychotherapy that address particular symptoms of BPD with success. One of the best-known all-encompassing BPD treatment plans is **Dialectical Behavior Therapy (DBT)**, developed by Marsha M. Linehan, PhD, at the University of Washington. DBT teaches skills to manage emotions, tolerate distress and improve relationships for a better balance or control. Dr. Linehan refers to BPD as a "dysregulation", therefore providing skills to regain regulation of behavior. DBT has been particularly effective in addressing the triggers for suicide and self-harming behaviors.

Cognitive-Behavioral Therapy (CBT), developed by Dr. Aaron Beck, identifies dysfunctional thinking and behavior and teaches skills to change this distorted thinking and troublesome behavior. This therapy is more concerned about the here and now.

Systems Training for Emotional Predictability and Problem Solving (STEPPS) was developed at the University of Iowa. STEPPS involves group therapy sessions with the BPD's social system members to understand and help the borderline's difficulties in normalizing their emotions and impulses.

Schema-Focused Therapy (SFT) was developed by Jeffrey Young, PhD. SFT focuses on identifying and changing specific unhealthy ways of thinking. When basic childhood needs are not met, it leads to unhealthy ways of thinking and behaving that relate to the past.

Mentalization-Based Therapy (MBT) studied by Peter Fonagy, PhD, helps to identify thoughts and feelings and to create different perspectives that empathizes with the feelings of another. Dr. Fonagy theorized that childhood development or interruption of mentalization effected adult thinking and feeling.

Transference-Focused Psychotherapy (TFP) was developed by Otto Kernberg, MD, is an approach to understand emotions and interpersonal difficulties by working with a therapist to examine identity diffusion and splitting.

As an adult, Kathy had been observed as demonstrating all nine symptoms of BPD. This book will describe incidents and thoughts during her lifetime, that are categorized as BPD symptoms. There is little to identify conclusive genetic influences as a basis for Kathy's Borderline Personality Disorder. However, there is a vestige of disclosure that mental illness and alcoholism were present in her family history. There is some doubt if Kathy knew the full extent of the emotional turmoil in her life, but she would have had to commit to change if psychotherapy, particularly Dr. Marsha Linehan's Dialectical Behavior Therapy (DBT), were to help her. She was making admirable progress with Alcohol Anonymous (AA), so perhaps she could have committed to DBT. Knowing Kathy, it would have been a long and difficult to path for her. This is her story.

10

My Birth Parents

My birth father was Theodore Richard Smith and my mother was Diane Louise Corbin. I did not know much about Ted Smith other than my mother met him while he was in the Navy and she had just graduated from Bellevue High School, Bellevue Washington, in 1961. They were married in 1961 or 1962. They were young, and Diane was in a difficult family situation growing up that led to her desire to leave home. They had a son, Charles Richard Smith in July 1962. I was born at 8:21 PM on July 21, 1963 at San Pedro Community Hospital, San Pedro, California, because Ted was stationed in San Diego. I was named Kathryn Colleen Smith. We lived in base housing and shortly after I was born, my parents separated and my mother, brother and I moved to Kirkland, Washington, where Diane had family support. It was a bitter separation. They were officially divorced on September 1, 1966, when Diane filed for divorce in Kitsap County, State of Washington.

As I stated, I did not know Ted Smith, but when they separated, it became my *first experience with abandonment*. It was not unusual for mother-daughter relationships to be strained but I think that I was born at a time of much distress for my mother. The lack of mother-daughter bonding during my early years, in my opinion, established the foundation for the relationship that existed throughout our lives. Charles, affectionately known as Chuck, was the favorite son and my arrival compounded the challenges for a young, single parent with financial problems which included Ted filing for bankruptcy and leaving my mother's name off the legal document filed with the court. Still married at that time meant that Diane was liable for joint debts.

I was told by my mother that Ted Smith's father was a chiropractor and that his wife had some mental issues, perhaps depression and bipolar symptoms. Ted's grandmother was a kind and caring individual. On Diane's side of the family, her mother, Florence was an alcoholic. Florence was a single parent with a good job at Boeing on the plant floor. Diane was the parent of her mother and there were numerous times when she would be looking in the window at the Central Tavern in Kirkland, Washington, trying to get the attention of her mother inside. Owners and patrons of the tavern knew Diane from the frequency of her need to get her mother home. Florence was a caring individual consumed by alcoholism. She died tragically from a head wound resulting from a fall in front of the house she rented. She was drunk and there was speculation, on Diane's part, that she was struck or pushed by a male friend. She died in Harborview Hospital in Seattle, Washington. There was no police investigation into the death. Diane's father, Clem Corbin and oldest brother could be described as fully functioning alcoholics. One of Diane's brothers, Raymond, died tragically in a single car accident on NE 85th Street in Kirkland, Washington, while under the influence of alcohol.

My Grade School Years

I wanted to share teacher feedback that I received in grade school to see if there were clues of Borderline Personality Disorder that were missed. There was feedback in the "satisfactory, making progress, etc.," category, but I am going to focus on comments that were less favorable or identifying areas where improvement was needed, fully recognizing that they are taken out of context.

I attended Lakeview Elementary School in Kirkland, Washington. Back in those days, we could ride a school bus, but we also walked to and from school. It was 1.5 miles one way and not usual for kids to walk to school, particularly if you missed the bus. The concerns we have today, causing parents to stand at the bus stop or wait in a car, before and after school, were not present in the 1970's. We did walk in small groups to keep each other in line and to have some security in numbers. Here are the comments that appeared on my progress reports in elementary school. I should say that I hated Fourth Grade Teacher B, and I really liked Fourth Grade Teacher A, Fifth Grade Teacher B and Sixth Grade Teacher B. Their comments probably reflected my biases.

> **4/8/1970, First Grade Teacher** wrote: "Kathy has shown improvement in using her work time better, although she still spends too much time talking when she should be working. She should listen more carefully while assignments are being explained, as she is still having difficulty following directions."

> **6/1970, First Grade Teacher** wrote: "Kathy has made a little more effort to use her work time better. She has been getting her assignments finished on time and they have been done more carefully. She still needs to be frequently reminded about unnecessary talking. She has a good attitude toward discipline and is very cooperative. She is an outgoing, active girl and gets along well with her classmates. Kathy wants to

take the easy way out as far as thinking through an assignment is concerned and needs to be encouraged to put forth more effort."

11/6/1970, Second Grade Teacher wrote: "Kathy sometimes tries to hurry through her assignments and the work has careless mistakes, as a result. She is able to use her work time well and stick with a job until it is done. She gets along well with her classmates and has a very cooperative attitude. Kathy is still not using phonics or context clues as much as she should be. She reads 'went' for 'want', etc.. This not only slows her down but causes her to miss the meaning of what she is reading. Very eager to join in games and plays very hard."

3/5/1971, Second Grade Teacher wrote: "Kathy has not been using her work time as well as she was, and often is not completing her assignments. I have told her that I want her to be responsible for her work and seeing that it gets handed in. However, I find I have to keep checking up on her. She also could put more effort into doing it carefully and correctly. She continues to have a positive attitude towards school and respects school rules."

6/1971, Second Grade Teacher wrote: "Kathy is still not using her independent work time as well as she should be. She spends too much time talking and doesn't get her work finished. Her work is not always carefully done, unless I keep checking on her. Kathy takes corrections well but should take more pride in doing a job well and take the responsibility for it herself. She is cooperative about obeying school rules and gets along well with her classmates."

11/19/1971, Third Grade Teacher wrote: "Kathryn does not always start her work promptly and in math doesn't always complete her work. Her work is neat. She is able to accept suggestions. Her citizenship is good. Participates in group PE, art and music activities."

3/1972, Third Grade Teacher wrote: "Her citizenship is good. She completes papers on time but usually hurries through putting down just any answer without thinking. Is a good listener most of the time.

11/7/1972, Fourth Grade Teacher A wrote: "Slow progress – needs more practice using words in more than one way. Slow progress following directions - not always certain of directions."

11/1972, Fourth Grade Teacher B wrote: "Talks too much. Tries to be helpful to others. Is a fine helper in the room clean-up."

4/1973, Fourth Grade Teacher B wrote: "Follows directions usually. Completes work not always on time. Sometimes contributes effectively to discussions. Explores art experiences creatively often at the expense of her classwork. Plays hard at all games. Sometimes finds it hard to accept group decisions."

6/8/1973, Fourth Grade Teacher A wrote: "Kathy has shown progress in her comprehension and is more sure of herself in oral discussion and recitation."

6/1973, Fourth Grade Teacher B wrote: "Is often too critical of others. Seldom contributes effectively to discussions. Social attitudes-sportsmanship-Short fuse."

11/1973, Fifth Grade Teacher A wrote: "I feel that Kathy could produce more than she does. She seems to spend some of her time in an unproductive manner. Kathy does have good ability and we are working on main ideas, soon to work on sequence."

11/1973, Fifth Grade Teacher B wrote: "She usually completes her assignments on time. Occasionally is impatient - needs to wait her turn and be more considerate."

11/1973, Fifth Grade Teacher C wrote: "Kathy has a hard time with some of her work, but she tries. Occasionally she is teased, but usually takes it fairly well.

3/1974, Fifth Grade Teacher C wrote: "Cheerful girl. Has a good attitude."

6/10/1974, Fifth Grade Teacher B wrote: "I have enjoyed working with Kathy. She is cooperative and very willing to do her best."

6/1974, Fifth Grade Teacher C wrote: "Good citizen. Being patrol captain for a week was quite trying for Kathy."

11/1974, Sixth Grade Teacher B wrote: "Kathy has shown good progress in all areas. She is getting along much better with her peers. Did a fine job with the play group. Very thoughtful and responsible patrol girl."

3/1975, Sixth Grade Teacher B wrote: "Kathy continues doing well in all growth areas. She contributes in all activities with a great deal of motivation and interest. Excellent effort as 'clue master'-selection and organizing-dependable. Conscientious patrol girl."

As I looked back at these grade school teacher comments, I realized that some of the significant comments did not support the full-fledged symptoms of BPD. However, there were observations of behavior that could be very early leanings at a young age. The common themes were a) too much talking, b) listen more carefully, c) difficulty following directions, d) careless mistakes, e) sometimes finds it hard to accept group decisions, f) too often critical of others – short fuse, g) occasionally is impatient – needs to wait her turn and be more considerate and h) occasionally she is teased but usually takes it fairly well. In and of itself, these comments did not seem alarming and could have appeared on many student progress reports of her age group. The contention is that these comments can loosely support the following BPD symptoms: **Abandonment or rejection; intense relationships; emotional swings; feelings of emptiness; and dissociative symptoms.** Admittedly, these comments do not rise to the degree of BPD symptoms that will be discussed in later adult years.

My Junior High School Years

I attended Rose Hill Junior High School in Redmond, Washington. My student reports during the junior high school years were unremarkable. While my grade school reports contained teacher comments on personal and social growth, these types of comments were less prominent after elementary school. I received a letter from a counselor at Rose Hill Junior High, congratulating me on my second trimester report card indicating "successful achievement as an excellent student…" My report card dated 6/16/1978, showed my current GPA as 2.835. My Stanford Achievement Test taken in April 1978, showed a battery total of 66 Percentile Rank and a Stanine Score 6 which placed me slightly above average. Here are some of the limited comments that were available.

> **7/1/1976, Seventh Grade Teacher A** wrote: "Listens while teacher and students are speaking sometimes. Well Behaved most of the time. Talks out of turn sometimes."

> **3/15/1977, Eighth Grade Teacher B** wrote: "Sometimes disruptive."

> **5/3/1977, Eighth Grade Teacher B** wrote: "Disturbs class occasionally. Works well in class-not always. Kathy sometimes needs to concentrate on getting her work done during the time provided in class rather than talking with others because it prevents them from doing their assigned work."

Junior high years are well documented as challenging times for early teens. There can be many factors affecting school performance such as raging hormones or newly found freedom and independence. However, in these limited teacher comments, there is a common behavioral theme of being disruptive. This can be associated with ***abandonment or rejection***. The BPD can be disruptive or sarcastic if they feel ignored or not the center of focus. This behavior can be to get attention or mask the feeling of not being included in the learning or activity of the class.

My High School Years

I attended Lake Washington High School in Kirkland, Washington. My Student Progress Reports were unremarkable but generally with good comments. The one exception was sophomore PE where I got a D grade because of excessive absences. Many of the Student Progress Reports were not available as I remember intercepting the mail, so my parents did not get them. At the end of my junior year, my accumulated GPA was 2.77. I remember that it had come down to the wire in my senior year as to whether I would have the credits necessary for graduation. I think I was one point over the required number just days before graduation.

More freedom and new friends in high school added another level of normal growing up. Working, having money, driving a car, and becoming more independent occurred in high school. Ironically, independence bred feelings of *abandonment* as you try to find your own way with behavior sometimes diametrically opposed to what your family or friends think you should do. The teenage years can be filled with **unstable personal relationships** where you love someone and then hate them. There can be **distorted or unstable feelings of self-image** whether they are based on looks, weight, personality, friends, grades, or whatever. There can be **feelings of depressed moods, irritability or anxiety, boredom, or anger** as a normal course of teenage years. Granted, the level of intensity of these feelings, as a part of teenage years, may not rise to the level of BPD symptoms and, frankly, are not that different from most teenagers.

My Childhood and Growing Up

A predominate theme of my childhood was the absence of my mother at home. I suppose it was the sign of the times. The days of couples staying together for the sake of the kids did not happen but that may not be so unusual given the bitter state of the separation of my parents. As a single parent with no spousal support financially, emotionally, or joint custody of the kids, it meant that my mother had to go to work full time and moonlight in a part-time job and still be a nurturing mother, housekeeper, chauffeur, school parent, etc. There are just not enough hours in a day or physical energy to do it all. **Abandonment.**

When we moved from San Pedro, California, after my parent's separation, my grandmother, Florence, watched us at her rental home on NE 70th Street in Kirkland, Washington. It was an older home and we played frequently in the basement. I remember the washer and dryer were in the basement and the floor was a black and white checked tile. It was a dark and dirty basement and it was creepy. As I look back, the basement was the type you would see in a movie scene where someone is held captive, tortured and killed. The washer and dryer provided a mechanism to clean up the mess. We took our naps on a bed with a large wooden headboard. There were ornate carvings on the headboard of a large bird or bat with its wings spread. I remember having nightmares of that bird coming to life and flying around the room like a vulture stalking its prey, me. I would wake up crying and shaking. **Feelings of anxiety and paranoia.**

Chuck and I spent a couple of years at the Buddy Bear House on NE 108th in Kirkland, Washington. This was a child care facility that had great street appeal as a wonderful place to leave your kid while parents went to work. Child care was a tough business. There were good kids who were easy to watch and there were ADHD (attention-deficit/hyperactivity disorder) kids who required more work. I remember two scarring incidents as clear as if they happened yesterday. The first incident occurred when my mother was late picking us up after work. No doubt that she was late because of an accident or stalled car on the 520 Evergreen Point Floating Bridge connecting Seattle with the Eastside. To punish us for our mother's tardiness, the lights were turned off in the facility and we were required to lay still on the cots. Laying on the cots in total darkness was a frightening experience and one that we would share with our mother to impress upon her that this can't happen again. The second incident involved a field trip to downtown Kirkland on the Buddy Bear House bus. There were about 20 kids and one by one they got on the bus. I was the last kid and just as I was about to board the bus, the coordinator stopped me and said that the bus was full and that I would not be going on the field trip. I was left to sit on a 'mat' all day while the other kids were gone. How does that make you feel? Poor me. **Abandonment.**

My mother used to tell everyone that "Patty" was such a wonderful baby sitter. Patty must have really "kissed up" to parents for them to feel so good about her work because she was mean. Patty's house was a couple of blocks east of downtown Kirkland, Washington. There were about 5 or 6 kids that Patty watched. We would go there after school, either walking there or taking the school bus over the course of 3 years. There were four incidents that were memorable to me beyond the daily crap we had to put up with. The first incident involved Patty's teenage son, Dick. There was a popular song by Shirley Ellis and Lincoln Chase titled "The Name Game". Dick was singing the song with all the kids and then he came to Chuck's name. We listened carefully and soon Chuck and I were enthusiastically singing along. The words that we were singing were "Chuck, Chuck, bo Bhuck, Banana-fana foe fuck, See-sigh so-suck, Chuck".

Patty heard us singing and she washed our mouths with a bar of soap and made us sit in the dark on some stairs as punishment for using a bad word. We were just singing and had no idea what the words meant. The second incident involved Patty's son, Dick again. There was a small inflatable wading pool in the backyard for warm summer afternoons. Dick was a mean and sadistic and he pushed my head under the water and held it there until I was able to struggle free. He thought it was funny to scare a little girl like me this way and to make a point to the other children. He was a real case and it would be interesting to know what kind of an adult he became. The third incident involved a bully kid a little older than me. He had his bicycle turned over and he told me to put my finger on the sprocket. Then, he turned the pedal and my finger got caught between the chain and the sprocket. I was crying, and my finger was bleeding and crooked. Patty came running when she heard the commotion and proceeded to yell at me for being so stupid to put my finger on the sprocket. I had to stand in the corner until my mom came to pick us up. The final incident did not involve us directly but left a significant impact on me. There was a brother and sister about the same age as Chuck and me. We had become friends with them because of our similar ages. One day, there was an accident on the 520 Evergreen Point Floating Bridge and it was their mother. She was killed in the accident and we never saw those kids again. I worried that someday my mother would face the same destiny and we would be orphaned. I watched the clock when it was near the time that she would be there to pick us up. It was constant fear. **Abandonment, rejection and self-harm.**

We lived in a modest 3-bedroom rambler in Kirkland, Washington with a good size lot. My mother bought the house for $12,500 and was able to make a down payment from the proceeds of a life insurance policy when her brother Ray died. We had nice neighbor kids including William, Don and Doris. They would always go to the Crescent Bar or Sun Lakes, in Eastern Washington in the summer and we were never invited. The neighbor kids up the hill were Dennis and Sam and their family had a place at Indianola, Washington, across Puget Sound, and we were invited there once. I guess this was a ***feeling of abandonment or rejection.*** I always felt jealous of them, but my mother tried hard to provide a vacation every summer despite of her limited income. We even went to Disneyland, the Oregon Coast and to Spokane, Washington, to visit our grandparents and cousins. She worked in payroll at the Seattle Center and moonlighted as a concessions worker on evenings and weekends for events at the Seattle Center (the 1962 World's Fair site) and the University of Washington Husky Stadium and Hec Edmundson Pavilion. Dennis and Sam's sisters would babysit us often while mom worked or went out. The mother of Dennis and Sam was a 'stay-at-home mom' who was always there for her kids unlike our mom. She also knew everything that was going on in the neighborhood and kind of kept an eye on us which was both good and bad. She would tell my mom when we did something bad.

All the neighborhood kids would spend hours in the "water shed" at the end of the street. This was a large wooded area that is a park with walking trails today. We played "hide and seek". My memories include being left behind and not included in the games. I was always tagging along behind the boys and trying to be included. It seemed like they were trying to ditch me. I felt bad and went home crying to my mother many times, ultimately getting Chuck in trouble. This meant he was forced to take me with him. Quite often I would be hysterical and sobbing as I told my mother what had happened. I felt a lot of resentment from this and my credibility was questioned quite often because of my hysterical state. I had feelings of **abandonment, uncontrollable anger and an unstable self-image**. I remember one time we were playing in the "water shed" like usual. Unbeknownst to us, there was a

"Breaking News" report on television that there was a man with a gun shooting at cars from a grassy knoll near the interchange and off ramp of State Route 520 and Interstate 405. There were State Patrol officers and Kirkland, Redmond and Bellevue police cars all over the place with their lights flashing. They had stopped all traffic on the two highways and were in pursuit of the shooter. The most logical place for the shooter to run and hide was the wooded "water shed" which was directly to the north of the grassy knoll. My mother was worried sick knowing that we were playing in the "water shed". Eventually, we came out of the woods of the "water shed" and were shocked to see all the police officers and cars with their lights flashing. It was then that we found out what was happening and how scary it was to be in those woods. I became even more emotional and hysterical when I saw how upset my mother was that we were in possible danger.

My mother had a long-term relationship with Gil Stratford who worked in management at Seattle Center. Gil watched us many evenings and weekends while mom worked her second job. His job required him to be on call and facilitated his ability to be with my mother during evenings and weekends. He helped us with homework and got us ready for bed. He made sure that we took a bath and were in bed by 8:00 pm. I remember Gil lying in bed with me when I had trouble falling asleep. He would read a short story and cuddle me to sleep. I don't remember if he molested me, but the opportunity was certainly there. Cases of **physical and sexual abuse** were common in the backgrounds of BPD patients. I remember my uncle always giving me and my brother "wedges" which was pulling up on the back of your underpants to the point of lifting you off your feet. Everyone thought it was funny, but it was very humiliating.

A strange thing happened one day when Gil was at a 'Indian Scouts" meeting with my brother Chuck. A man approached him and called him Ben. Evidently, he had met Ben at the Seattle Center. Gil responded that his name was Gil Stratford but that did not dissuade this other parent. The truth was out. Gil was Ben and he was married and living a dual life. The seven-year relationship between Gil and my mother ended shortly afterward in a loud and heated breakup at work over Gil's new affair with a young intern. I remember my mother was crying for days after the breakup and very emotionally saddened. As a child, you do get close to someone after seven years, so this was another case for "*abandonment*".

In the summer of 1972, we were on a vacation at a cabin at Lake Heritage, north of Spokane, Washington, with our grandfather Clem and his wife, Claudia. I was cleaning a fish with my grandfather's knife and cut my finger right at the base of my baby finger. It hardly bled and was not a deep cut. A few days later, I noticed that I could not move my baby finger. The doctor determined that I had cut the tendon at the base of the finger and that surgery was needed. The doctor reattached the tendon and my hand and arm to the elbow were in a hard cast. It was warm and itchy under the cast, so I stuck pencils inside to scratch. Eventually, I broke off pieces of the cast to provide comfort to my arm and hand. When we returned for a follow-up visit with the doctor, he determined that the tendon had separated, and another surgery would be required. This time a tendon was removed from my foot and grafted to the tendon at base of my finger. So now I had a cast on my foot and my arm. I was not happy spending my summer in this condition and unfortunately, I managed to fight with the cast again and ultimately, the second surgery, compounded by scar tissue, failed. This could be interpreted as an early sign of *"**self-harming behavior**"*.

Also, in the summer of 1972, my mother met Jimmy who worked at Seattle Center. Over the course of the next year, we were very much like a family. My bedroom was painted pink and then one day, Chuck and I got a bunk bed and one of the bedrooms became a TV room. I remember we went to an auction in Renton, Washington, and bought an orange couch for $20 for us to watch TV. Jimmy helped us with school homework and projects. One project that I remember well was that he and I baked a cake and shaped it into a toilet. The bowl and the tank were held together with toothpicks and it was appropriately frosted. Everyone in class was impressed with our creation and I won a ribbon for the "most original" baked item.

In July of 1973, Jimmy and my mother got married in Reno, Nevada. Chuck and I stayed with family friends during the few days that they were gone. I remember wondering what changes we would be facing with a new step-father. It had been a year that they were dating so as it turned out not much changed at all. My mother was still the disciplinarian and our financial state improved with the two incomes. Jimmy's family was nice to us, especially his mom and dad. They did their best to make us feel a part of the family. I'll be honest in saying that there was a twinge of a **"feeling of abandonment"** as we now shared our mother, who for me, was all that I was attached to. By the Fall of 1973, legal documents to adopt me and Chuck had been prepared by an attorney. When the notification and waiting period had elapsed, I changed my name to Kathy Yoko Kamada and my brother changed his name to Charles David Kamada. I chose my middle name "Yoko" because of the popularity of John Lennon and Yoko Ono from the Beatles fame and it would be a Japanese middle name. This may have represented some **"abandonment feelings"** as I was losing a birth name and birth family, although I had not had any contact with my birth father. There had been no birthday or

Christmas cards or presents. I do have to say that that was what my mother had insisted upon. She was very bitter toward our birth father and her actions or absence of any conciliatory moves were clearly indicative of such. It was interesting that with one legal move, our birth certificates were changed to show our father as Jimmy, age 18 and a student.

In May 1974, I gave my mother a handmade Mother's Day card. A seal on the folded paper states: "I expect to pass through this world but once. Any good thing, therefore, that I can do or any kindness I can show to any fellow human being – let me do it now. Let me not deter nor neglect it, for I shall not pass this way again". A handkerchief with a flower drawn with magic markers was enclosed.

Growing up, I was active in sports, skiing, swimming, and soccer. I was a pretty good soccer player and goalie. I was fiercely competitive, and my soccer hero would have been Hope Solo (two-time Olympic gold medalist and World Cup Champion) if she were playing when I was young. I was not afraid to dive for the ball, crash into an on-coming opponent or to intimidate anyone. I remember a time at the Peter Kirk Swimming Pool in Kirkland, Washington, on the last day of swimming lessons. There was a contest to determine who could swim the farthest. Chuck swam the full length of the pool and appeared to be the winner. It was now my turn and I swam the full length, touched the edge and turned around and swam back. The parents cheered and applauded that I had swam the furthest. I always had to get the last "dig in". Go Girl!

I think I had a normal childhood with vacations, summer camps and many holiday gatherings. I always got what I wanted for my birthday and Christmas. I don't think it was very different than most of my friends. I was a tomboy and played mostly with boys in competitive games. The girl friends that I had were soccer or softball teammates and those friendships did not grow beyond being fellow team players.

I had a unique ability to size up someone within minutes and zero in on their character vulnerabilities. I could bend, stretch and shade with irony someone's character flaws with true comedic talent and channel it correctly for maximum wit and humor. It was an unbelievable gift and I could use mockery to make anyone a little sad and mad. This was a talent that I used my entire life and no doubt affected my ability to make lasting friends. I could be very critical and judgmental. My comments could seem funny and would make people laugh, but in fact they were hurtful and cutting to the recipient. This ability was noted as a BPD characteristic.

I do remember a terrifying incident that exemplified "*abandonment*". We were on the ferry going to Bainbridge Island, Washington. Chuck and I had left the car to go to the restroom and explore the passenger deck of the ferry. I heard the announcement that the ferry was approaching the dock and that passengers were reminded to return to their cars. Chuck and I were separated, and I was distracted by the view of the beach as we neared the dock. The next thing I remember was that I was standing on the outside passenger deck as the cars were driving off the ferry. I saw our car driving off of the ferry and I saw my family looking up and seeing me. I was horrified and hysterical and crying. I thought for sure that they were leaving me. My parents thought it was funny and a learning moment for me. Obviously, they pulled the car over at the first available opportunity and came running to get me. I was scared and felt intense fear of being left behind, not only from the ferry but from my family.

In June 1975, we moved to the Rose Hill neighborhood in Kirkland, Washington. This meant a new school and new friends. To help in the transition, the move resulted in getting my own room and new bedroom furniture. That was a first. It was unfinished furniture and I was able to help with the staining and varnishing. The new house, a split-level with a full basement, was larger and there was more room to find individual space. Then, our spacious living got a little smaller. My mother's aunt, Pat, moved in with us. Her husband had died suddenly from a heart attack and she was struggling financially as a widow. The family dynamics changed, and it was a difficult arrangement for all concerned. After about a year, Aunt Pat moved back to West Seattle into low rent housing and worked part-time at a local, dry cleaning shop. Aunt Pat did give us Christmas and birthday presents while we were growing up, so she wasn't all bad.

In September 1976, a new baby brother, Jeff, entered the family. Chuck and I were the central focus for my mother, and now she was a new mother. My parents made every effort to ensure that we were not stuck as baby-sitters for Jeff. On the surface, it seemed that Jeff's entrance to the family was working without major problems. I liked Jeff and enjoyed entertaining him when asked. But this was a period of many changes in my life, not the least of which was the confusing and challenging times of teenage years. This was a time of significant changes, socially and physiologically. The process of becoming more individualistic and independent was starting.

I guess it was at this point that I wanted to be a nurse. I falsified my birth month on my application for a job as a nursing aid at Cascade Vista Nursing Home, in Kirkland, Washington. I got the job and started earning money and became more independent. Money, independence, less focus at home, new friends, drugs, alcohol, sex and freedom, all meant life was changing.

My life in high school began in September 1978. Again, there were new friends, parties, and work. I met two sisters my age who worked at the nursing home and they lived just around the corner from my house. I spent a lot of time with them. Also, I met two special friends who would be close to me for life. One was John Jones who was gay before it was accepted as it is today. John and I were peas of the same pod. We were like twins in how we thought, spoke and acted. It was like we were soulmates. We enjoyed each other's company, we went places as a couple, and we were always together. We had disagreements and fought but always made up and life went on as if it never happened. The funny thing was that we even kind of looked alike. Years later, John overdosed on drugs and it was considered a death by suicide. I would have to say I was not surprised but it was a profound loss for me. I could count my close friends on one hand so to lose John was devastating. I found the most comfort in talking with John's mother because I felt she knew how close John and I were. **Abandonment and emptiness.**

My other life-long friend was Sheila. In some ways, we were different and yet very much alike. We were always together going to parties and hanging out. Sheila was very attractive and opened the doors for me to meet people and go parties. It was clear that Sheila was a female Eddie Haskell of the TV show "Leave it to Beaver" (a TV Series from 1957-1963). She was very personable and polite with my parents but just "full of it" when we were out on the town. I remembered one time we were eating a breakfast at Denny's late at night and we did not have money for the bill. We planned to make a run for it, but we were later caught and charged with theft. We thought it was just having fun and laughed it off with no remorse. My parents found out about it by reading the police blotter in the local Redmond newspaper. **Impulsive behavior.**

I remembered an occasion when my parents and grandparents were going across Puget Sound to pre-visit a camp that my brother Jeff was going to attend the next week. My grandmother made a Japanese bento for the outing. Sheila and I were hungover from the night before, but we decided that we wanted to go.

I don't think we were invited. My parents drove our motorhome, so everyone could travel together and have a place to eat. Sheila and I slept the whole way there and back including on the ferry. We were obnoxious the whole trip. I felt that my parents were ticked off with our behavior and lack of interaction. We didn't care and just laughed, oblivious of the feelings of my parents.

High school meant driving a car. I bought the family car, a blue, four door Datsun 610. I made payments to my parents every week from my paycheck from the nursing home. This was the first time I borrowed a sizable amount of money from my parents. I made all the payments except toward the end when I negotiated a payoff as a birthday or Christmas present. There were not very many of my friends who owned a car in high school. It helped my popularity and I guess I got used as a driver by some students too. They considered me their friend and that made it worth it.

As I mentioned earlier, I struggled in high school, but I was working a lot of hours at Cascade Vista and enjoyed the money. It seemed like I just didn't have enough time for all that was required. My home life was suffering too. I wasn't doing much around the house and I was constantly "yelled at" for not cleaning my room and making my bed. My room was a mess usually but like I said, there was no extra time. I went to see my counselor, Karen Siggaway, because I felt stressed with my life at home. Ms. Siggaway was my Physical Education teacher in my sophomore year, so she was concerned about a possible abusive situation. She was concerned that I had excessive absences from PE. Ms. Siggaway also knew that I could be emotional, hysterical and one-sided in PE classes. I told her that my home life was miserable, and my adoptive father was mean and yelled at me. Ms. Siggaway set up separate, individual meetings with my mother and my adoptive father to investigate my claims.

My mother told Ms. Siggaway that I was being an incorrigible teenager and that our family life was in turmoil as a result. My adoptive father described the watershed yelling incident when he angrily told me to clean up my room and left me crying. It seemed like there were many times when I was hysterical and sobbing. Ms. Siggaway completed her investigation and met with my parents to discuss her conclusions. She recommended counseling for me and that a foster home could be the solution to reduce the stress on the family. I was shocked at the recommendation but glad that my parents decided to try and make things work. I think Ms. Siggaway knew that I could be difficult, after all she gave me a "D" for PE. **Extreme emotional swings.**

I begged and begged my parents to let me have a party at the house. They rejected my initial request but ultimately agreed with some conditions. They would stay upstairs and not come downstairs and the party would end at midnight. The party was typical of most teenager house parties, loud music, rowdy kids, drugs, alcohol and worried parents. We were lucky in that damage to the house was minimal but mischievous. Back in the 1970's, it was common to have a mirror with an attached, small sliding door steel cabinet below it in the bathroom like we had. Some partygoer(s) decided it would be funny to pour liquid hand soap into the bottom of the cabinet. That did not seem like such a terrible thing to do. Kids being kids, right? Just clean it up, right? Wrong. That little prank lived on for a long time. Every time you took a shower and the room steamed up, the cabinet bubbled, dripped soap and finally rusted.

A few weeks after the party, I told my mother that I had been raped by a boy who was at the party. My mother was skeptical because the details were sketchy and incomplete. I think she thought it was two teenagers getting caught up in a moment under the influence of drugs or alcohol. As luck would have it, I was pregnant and eventually I had an abortion, the first of two. **Abandonment, unstable self-image and emotions and emptiness.**

During my senior year, I decided to contact my birth father, Ted Smith. My parents asked that I wait until after I graduated and then they would give me their blessing. But, a popular song by Lesley Gore, "It's My Party" at the time reflected how I felt. I changed the lyrics to be "it's my life and I can do whatever I want to, do whatever, I want to" and sang it to the melody of that song. And so, against the wishes of my parents, I invited Ted Smith to my graduation ceremony and to the afterparty at the house. My mother was livid, and my adoptive father tried to be civil. The evening passed without an incident although it must have been traumatic for my mother based on the bitter feelings from the bankruptcy, divorce and lack of any child support. I even went down to California to visit my birth father for a week at his home. His wife and family were nice to me and I had an enjoyable vacation. I had a couple of other contacts with him and he offered to pay for my higher education. That never happened. When the time came to go to community college to study nursing, there was no financial assistance, and my contact with him pretty much ended. **Abandonment, intense relationships, emotional swings, and emptiness.**

My Young Adult Life

Within a month of graduation, I moved out of the house. I was so happy to be on my own and to be my own boss. I thought my parents were happy too and they helped me move. I really had a knack for decorating my room and now I had an apartment to decorate in downtown Kirkland, Washington. I was in heaven. Later, I moved to a house in Kirkland, Washington, and then another apartment in Lake Forest Park in Seattle, Washington. These last two living arrangements were with male roommates. I got along with male roommates because I could drink, swear, bully and ridicule with the best of them. I was pretty much working most of the time and trying to keep up with bills. I did not have to listen to anyone, especially my parents, and I could live my life however I wanted.

In 1981-82, I played on the Virginia Mason Hospital employee's softball team. I was pretty good at sports and I was the catcher for the team. In one game, I hit what was to be a home run, and as I was rounding third base, the player on the other team tripped me. I fell awkwardly and twisted my knee. It hurt like nothing I had ever felt before. The team assistant coach took me to Virginia Mason Hospital and the doctors diagnosed the injury as an anterior cruciate ligament grade 3 meniscal tear. Surgery was scheduled, and I would be off work for six to eight weeks. Virginia Mason Hospital was very accommodating at first as it was an employer sponsored game but after the normal disability period ended and paid leave stopped, I was on unpaid leave. After a few more weeks, I was terminated. This incident was ironic because it was similar to an incident at an annual family picnic. We were playing a softball game and my father was on one team and I was on the other team. He hit a home run and was rounding third base and jawing at me in jest, so I tripped him. He fell hard seriously scraping his knees and elbows. They were bleeding profusely and all the players on both sides came running to render aid. All I could do was laugh at what had happened and I could feel everyone was shocked at my insensitive behavior. **Unstable emotional swings and a dissociative symptom.**

In April 1983, I sent this card to my mother and the card read:

> Oh, well. Another year, another wrinkle! Happy Birthday!
> I wrote: "Mom – Happy 40th! Love your darling Daughter, Kathy XXOOXX"

I remembered one summer going camping at the State Park on Lake Chelan, Washington, and meeting up with my parents and my brother, and his two kids. My brother and I were getting along but mostly when we were sharing a joint. I had brought my motor scooter along on the back of my truck. Everyone was having fun riding it around the Park grounds. I was Aunt Kathy and gave Chuck's kids rides on the scooter. Chuck decided to drive the scooter, without asking, to take his laundry to the laundromat. I told him "no" and a big shouting match ensued. My mother was upset and sided with my brother. That was all I could take, and I packed up my things, put my motor scooter on my truck and drove off without saying a word. Fuck them all, I said to myself as I headed home. **Abandonment, intense relationships, explosive anger and dissociative symptoms.**

On Easter 1984, I sent this card that read:

> For both of you Mother and Dad at Easter –
> For Mother...A loving wish that Easter and each day all year through will bring a lot of happiness, Mother, just for you! For Dad...Hope Easter time and springtime bring everything that's glad to make you very happy. For you deserve it. Dad.
> **I wrote** *"Mom and Jimmy, sorry no B-day present, but times are tuff! Love ya, Kathy XXXOOO"*

In April 1984, I sent a card that read:

> For a wonderful mother on her birthday. For all your giving, all your caring, all your loving, too – This brings a lot of thanks, Mother…and a world of love for you!
>
> **I wrote: "*Mom, Happy #41 Birthday. I'll bring you a birthday surprise next time I'm in Seattle. Happy Birthday. Love ya very much, Kathy XXXOOO*"**

In June 1984, I sent a note written to my father.

> **I wrote: *"Yesterday I was forced to decide whether or not to get you a Hallmark card or to have just one more teeny-weeny little beer at the local Kirkland pub. GUESS WHAT? Happy Father's Day! Love your daughter, Kat XXXOOO"***

In May 1985, while I was at Western Washington University in Bellingham, Washington, I sent a card to my mother that read:

(A picture of Lucy of Peanuts on the cover)

I wanted to get you something really special for Mother's Day. But then I realized, what could be more special than a kid like me?

I wrote: "Like the card says – money can't buy an already perfect gift...me! (especially when this perfect little gift is on a college budget!) Have a good day – (you deserve it) Love, Kathy

Thanks for paying for my parking ticket but I already paid for it a couple of months ago. However, I did notice that the particular check did not go through. But if you are interested in paying more bills, I have a $22.00 phone bill that would love some attention. Love, Kathy!"

In July 1985, I sent a birthday card to my father. The card read:

> Dad, is there anything I can help you with on your Birthday? Can I clean out the garage? Can I clean out the basement? Your Pockets? Your Wallet? Happy Birthday!"
>
> **I wrote: "*Jimmy - (just let me know when you need any help!) Love, Kathy XOXO*"**

While not conclusive, the messages on these cards and my personal notes showed signs of ***emotional swings and sarcasm***.

My First Marriage

In February 1987, I sent this card to my mother. The card read:

> Damned if you do. Damned if you don't. C'mom, c'mom-it's either one or the other. **I wrote: "I'd say 'Life's a bitch' and 'then you die' but I think the saying 'Life's a virgin and then you die' – It's more appropriate because being a bitch is too easy. Oh well I hope you're not feeling sad any more, PMS or not! Love, Kathy XXXOOOXXX"** **Intense anger and sarcasm.**

In April 1987, I sent a card to my mother that read:

> I would climb the highest mountain to wish you Happy Birthday, Mom! Happy Birthday, Mom.
> **I wrote: *"Mom, sorry I couldn't be there. Love, Kathy" Emotional swing.***

I met my first husband-to-be in a downtown Seattle bar on 1st Avenue. His name was Bill Shipman and he was visiting his mother and family in Granite Falls, Washington, from Alaska. Bill was a diminutive, muscular man who grew up in the "Bush" in Alaska. He was a self-made, industrious, intelligent and mechanically oriented man. Bill was polite, articulate, well-read and was home taught. Socially, the effects of growing up in the "Alaskan Bush" had to be a major cultural shift from the Seattle bar scene. After dating for a short time, I was expecting and on July 26, 1987, we had a son, Craig.

In October 1987, I went to the Alaskan Bush for the first time. I wrote this progressive letter to my parents with the last entry on November 3, 1987:

> **Dear Mom, Jimmy and Jeff –**
> **It's been a month since Bill, Craig and I arrived in the Bush of Alaska. It's been a wonderful, interesting, boring, tiring and trying time for all of us, and the city will be a sight for sore eyes when we finally get there. We will begin to try and get out on Saturday and with any luck will be in Fairbanks in a week or so. Of course, this letter won't be mailed until we get**

into McGrath, so I'll try and write about things that I'll fail to mention on the phone.

The day we flew in we travelled 12 miles up river via canoe. How does one travel up river in a canoe? We had a motor that we could use at times, but mainly we were pulled by Bill and his brother, Aaron by a rope that was tied on the canoe. We went about three miles the first night and camped out on the edge of the river bank without a tent, a motorhome or anything. Bill made us a spruce branch bed and we weathered the cold until morning. The moon was full that night and we could hear a pack of wild wolves in the distance and a beaver swimming about 100 yards away up river. The beaver was flapping his tail up and down which Aaron said was warning to us not to get too close to his house.

It took us about eight more hours the next day to get to the homestead at which we saw beaver, otter, moose and beautiful country.

Bill has a wonderful family. His mom is real talkative and friendly and a "Christian". She's 40 years old but looks really, young for her age. She made Craig a pair of Marten booties (we know Marten as Sable in the States) as a gift that are really neat. She taught me how to sew and I made Craig a beaver hat that I think you'll be quite impressed with.

Bill's brothers, Aaron (15), Eli (11), and Derek (6) are all really, neat kids. Aaron acts much older than 15 and does much of the hard work around the homestead. You can imagine how much wood that needs to be cut to keep a cook stove and heating stove going all day. Bill has helped do all of that kind of work and much

more since we got here. He put a roof on our cabin which took about three days
and he finished making a pantry for his mother yesterday. Back to Aaron, on top of all his chores, he teaches himself school and runs a 15-mile trap line. He traps mainly for marten since their fur is worth the most. A marten is about the size of a small cat and their fur is worth anywhere from $60.00 to $100.00 depending on size and color. Besides it only takes about 15 minutes to skin marten where as a beaver skin is only worth about $30.00 to $50.00 and it takes about 4 hours to skin one. So, Aaron traps for beaver and otter mainly for the sport of it. Often, they will keep those furs and make hats and mittens out of them. Bill's mom could sell a pair of beaver mittens for $150.00 to $200.00. Aaron is the hunter of the family. He got all three of their moose this season and that is what we eat every day. Yesterday, little Derek

and I went with Aaron to check his beaver traps. Bill's mom said, "If Derek gets cold put the flaps to his hat down to cover his face." And then Bill said "Aaron, if Kathy gets too cold, run her". Brat! Bill said his father often used to talk about running a fat farm out in the woods. He said we would walk 'em for miles and miles and then just give them a few scraps of moose meat for dinner and charge them each $100.00. I tell ya, it would work too. Walking even two miles in the muskeg is hard work. You can only walk about a mile in an hour (my speed). I walk at least two miles every other day and a couple of times we walk six miles. Bill and I hiked this "hill" one day which was about three miles round trip, but it was a bitch. It was not my idea of a good time. Bill's real good about getting me out because I was getting cabin fever really bad hanging around his mother all day. She is a nice lady, but a month is too long to spend with in-laws.

Eli, who is Jeffrey's age is Craig's favorite. He's really good with Craig and really looks like him. Eli has made himself a log cabin fort that we have taken a picture of that you won't believe an 11 year-old could make. Carol (Bill's mom) thinks like Bill, Eli won't stay out in the woods. Whereas, Aaron probably will. Eli is in the 5th grade and struggling through school. If you can imagine, he is even a worse speller than I was at that age. He really has a hard time with it. All in all, he's a good kid and their most troubled.

Derek, the baby, is just a little cutie. He will talk your ear off if you let him. Each kid has a little trap line, Eli's is about three miles and Derek's is about a mile.

Frank, Bill's dad, is a hard man to handle. Fortunately, his trap line is about 60 miles and we don't see him too much now that trapping season has started. Like I have said to Bill, "Your family is all pretty normal except your Dad". Bill agrees and said that his Dad has said for years that he isn't normal and doesn't want to be. Frank loves Craig and he's nice enough. But, he has a terrible temper so much so that 10 years would be too soon for me to want to visit him again. Bill said that even with his temper he has never lay a hand on any of his kids. But if looks and words could kill, he would be a mass murderer. Bill would be really upset if he knew I gave such a one-sided impression of his Dad, but I have little respect for him though I don't treat him as such.

All in all, they are really, nice people, but like I said a month is just too long to spend with in-

laws. It's been too long for Bill. We are really looking forward to getting out of here, so we can get on with our plans for the future.

We've talked a lot about getting a piece of land and building a modern log home on it. Bill wants to build it himself, getting a logging permit to cut his own logs. He promises me that I'll have a shower, running water, and a washer and dryer and so I'll be a happy camper. (He wants those things too!) It all seems a dream right now but it's something that he considered a short-term goal.

Bill asked me to marry him, and despite everything I said about waiting, I said yes. We don't know when or where, but we do know that we love each other a lot.

Bill is a great man and I feel really, lucky to have him in my life. We really want Craig to be brought up in a committed relationship. We also did a lot of reflecting on the past year and decided that our relationship was much stronger than we ever thought, with all the ups and downs that we have already managed to live through. I'm not trying to sound like I'm convincing you he's the right man for me because I know he is. I love him very much, and he loves me.

Last, but not least – about your grandson! Craig has been a happy camper throughout the trip. He truly is a good boy! We started feeding him cereal and other foods gradually since we got out here. He's a real, good eater. He did have an allergic reaction to oatmeal though. We give him a bottle everyday which was a fight at first but now he takes it with no problem.

He's not particularly fond of formula so we started giving him Carnation instant milk and he loves it. (weird huh!) He didn't have any reaction to cow's milk though I know he could not live on that without some sort of fat supplement.

He's getting more hair slowly, but surely, and is as cute as ever. He has found his hand and feet and is really, quite active at reaching for things. I think he's gonna do fine at babysitters. Bill has made me quit nursing him to sleep and made him cry himself to sleep. He has never cried more than 10 minutes before he falls asleep. A lot of times, he won't even cry he just falls asleep. He still gets up once during the night but goes right back to sleep after he nurses.

Speaking of the little darling – he just woke up, so I better end this letter.

Looking forward to seeing you all again and getting back to the hustle and bustle of the city. Enclosed is a big, wet kiss from Craig. Love, always, Kathy XXXOOOXXX

This was the longest letter I had ever written in my life. As mixed as some of my messages were in the letter, this was a very memorable time in my life. I couldn't buy things, and so I made things. I didn't go out for fast foods because there were none. We had to shoot, trap or catch our food. I lost weight and was physically in the best shape of my life. Life was good. Sure, I started to feel the pressure of my in-laws but that would be pretty much normal for anyone. This was a time in my life where I think I was closest to portraying a non-BPD person.

October 4, 1987 — I sent this card to my parents. The card read:

> Just wanted to say Hello from McGrath, Alaska. I wrote: "*Dear Jimmy, Mom and Jeff, Its Sunday and we still haven't left McGrath, because the weather was too rotten yesterday. Today is beautiful though so we're planning on getting out today. Now we're waiting on the Bush pilot to get his act together. He's the kinda guy that does things when he wants to do them, so I don't know what time today we will get out. We bought supplies yesterday which totaled about $800.00, which Bill said was nothing. He said you should of seen when his family went into Fairbanks for 'yearly' supplies and bought 100's of pounds of sugar, flour, rice, etc.. It sure was fun. We stayed with some friends of Bill's last night instead of that expensive 'hotel'. God what a rip off that was. Expensive eating too. It*

cost $20.00 just for one breakfast. Later – Well Bob decided that it was too dangerous to fly out of McGrath on a float plane, so we are back to plan two. Take another plane farther down the river near his parent's place. This plane has wheels. If we would have just done this originally, we could have gone a couple of days ago. I'm starting to get slightly annoyed. Now we won't leave until tomorrow. I got to see the Northern Lights – they were so cool. It looked just like a light show at lazarium. It's moose season right now so you see dead moose all over the place. Moose meat taste so good. Much better than beef. Hanging moose meat in a shed outside will keep the meat all winter long. One moose will feed one person all year – (a good size bull moose). McGrath is a village of about 500 people whose size hasn't changed in the past 50 years. There are very few cars here, mostly 3-wheels and 4-wheels vehicles. They *call them 'machines'. Buffy, the guy Bill worked with in the mine, calls his machine, Jason, from the movie Halloween. It's supposed to be the best the 3-wheeler in the state. Yesterday, Bill took off my hat and glasses and told Buffy to take me for a ride. Last thing I heard was 'hang on' and I was taken for the ride of my life. We went about a mile down the road and doing a wheelie and then started riding on our side. It was better than any ride ever in Disneyland – also dangerous as hell. We went to a benefit dinner the other night to help this guy with an enlarged heart. I guess there is a lot of things like that that happen, because so many people can't afford medical care. I met the guy that shot Bill a few years ago. Bill doesn't like him at all anymore. Not because of the accident, but because he's a jerk. This is kinda an ugly card but there's not a lot of selection. There are only three stores and only*

> *one of them sells cards. Well, I'll close for now and write to John Jones. Talk to you as soon as I can. Love Kathy"*

In May 1988, I sent this card that read:

> Thanks, Mom...for everything! Happy Mother's Day with Love. **I wrote: *"Love, Kathy and Bill XXXOOOXXX"***

We were now living in a mobile home in Maltby, Washington. My mother was spending a good amount of time watching Craig. In fact, my mother had watched Craig all throughout his childhood years. Bill was working as a small engine mechanic and I was doing certified nursing jobs. I have been working toward becoming a registered nurse, taking classes at Bellevue Community College. Bill and I decided to get married in a hot air balloon over the Woodinville, Washington valley. There was a problem during the flight with some guide wires but it all ended up without a major calamity. It did not take too long before the "real calamity" happened. We were two, young and very different people starting to feel the pressures of marriage and parenthood. I was spending too much money and demanding this and that. Bill was feeling the loss of the independence he grew up with in the Bush. He was feeling like a trapped animal. The strained relationship and the pressure of being parents soon resulted in separation and divorce. Bill had difficulty adjusting to city life and bolted back to Alaska to return to work in the gold mines. With no child support, I was left with no option but to legally file for child support, and when he failed to appear at the court hearing, a warrant for his arrest was issued. That pretty much assured that he was not going to return anytime soon. ***Intense relationships, impulsive, self-destructive behavior and intense anger.***

My First House

I was living in an apartment in West Seattle. It was an older four-story building on a busy street not far from the West Seattle Junction. My roommate was a funny and a little weird black woman about the same age as me. She worked at CHEC Medical Center where I was working at the time. The weird part was she moonlighted as a phone sex operator. It was funny watching her talk dirty to creepy men who called her number. The money was good, and I even tried it once, but I was nowhere near as convincing as she was.

I believe it was the Fourth of July 1989, I was working a nursing shift, and my parents took Craig on a mini vacation over the Fourth in their motorhome. Craig was in his "terrible two's" and it had been a long weekend trip. When dropping off my brother Jeff's friend in Kirkland, Washington, Craig fell off the front seat and hit his head on a toolbox between the seats. He cried briefly and had a cut on his forehead that appeared to need a stitch or two. My parents put a band aid on it. I got a call from my mother about the accident and, told her to wait until I finished my shift and I would check it out. At my parent's house, they were busy unloading the motorhome and Craig took off down the street. My mother reprimanded him but within a few minutes, Craig started to run down the hill toward the busy street at the end of the block. My mother ran to catch up with him, and she grabbed his arm to pull him back. A couple of hours later, my mother noticed that Craig didn't appear to be using his arm. It was limp and hanging to his side. My mother called me to describe the situation, and I had seen cases where a child's elbow gets dislocated. I told my mother that my shift was almost over, and that I would check it out when I got there.

When I saw Craig, I determined that he could use a stitch or two on his forehead and that his elbow was dislocated. We headed to Evergreen Hospital in

Kirkland, Washington. We were in the Emergency Room waiting area, and Craig was getting cranky because it was now 9:30 PM. I gave my brother, Jeff some money to go to the vending machine to get a gum ball. Jeff came back with two red gum balls and my father asked, "are you sure that Craig can eat those?". I responded "yeah" he has had them before. Within a couple of minutes, Craig was choking and turning blue. I froze, and my mother summoned a nurse from behind the door. The nurse began the Heimlich maneuver and he appeared to be okay. The nurse returned behind the door, and then all of a sudden, Craig was choking again and turning blue. The nurse was called again and, repeated the Heimlich maneuver and Craig began to get his color back. So here was Craig with a cut on his head, an arm that does not move and experiencing the trauma of nearing choking to death, fortunately in the ER. The nurse felt the urgency of getting Craig to the examining room and asked me and my mother to come as well. While they were treating Craig, a social worker came in to question us about what had caused Craig's injuries. The social worker was actually conducting an investigation for possible child abuse. We all chuckled later about the unusual set of circumstances that led up to this unfortunate evening. **Dissociative symptoms under stress.**

While driving around West Seattle in September 1992, I stumbled upon an old, pre-World War II house on a large lot. The house had built-on additions, but it was still a small living space with an unfinished basement. Because of the large lot with an alley in back, it had a lot of potential. That house and lot would probably sell for $500,000 in today's market and would be an immediate teardown. The replacement house would be worth close to a million dollars. The house was a private owner sale and I figured out that I could use the $5,000 that my parents were going to give me when they received a reparation check from the US Government for the Japanese American internment. It would be 13 months before they received the check, but I needed the money now to close on the house, so they ended up borrowing $17,000 so I could buy the house. I said that I would pay them back, but I never did being a single parent struggling to make ends meet. My father and brother, Jeff built a fence around the front and sides of the lot to keep the dog fenced in and, also fixed up the basement for extra living and storage space. **Impulsive behavior.**

I was always good at making and selling a "financial plan" for major purchases. I made one when I bought my first car and now for my first house. Unfortunately, I was overly optimistic about my income sources (I could always work overtime, I thought) and grossly underestimated my expenses. What sounded like good financial plan on paper rarely made it to the end as expected. My parents were usually on the short end of the loan payments. I always felt that I needed to be living at the same financial level of my parents which was ridiculous since they both worked at good paying jobs. If they bought a TV, I needed to buy one. They gave many presents for birthdays and Christmas, and I needed to keep up by showering Craig with everything he wanted. When my mother bought a ¾ basset hound, I bought a full-blooded basset. If they had a cat, I had a cat. They had a parakeet and I got a bird. The difference was when I no longer wanted or could care for the animal, I got rid of it. I remember dropping off my cat in a vacant lot and my basset on the street. I did watch the basset until I saw a lady take it home. A year later, I saw the basset that I had loved but treated badly at times. I went up to the dog and the basset ignored me. No surprise there. **Impulsive behavior and intense animal relationships.**

There were some good times at my first house. I remembered having Craig's birthday party in the yard. My father's family and my grandmother's brother and his granddaughter from Japan came to the party. This was their first American birthday party complete with a piñata hanging from the tree and a wooden gym/swing set to play on. It looked like a Norman Rockwell painting of a happy birthday party. Good times don't seem to last forever for me. Craig was having difficulties adjusting to his new school. He wasn't making friends and his teachers felt he was not trying to do his best. I think that Craig was bored and more interested in video games which he had become quite good at. I decided that we were not West Seattle type people, and that we needed to return to our roots on the Eastside. **Impulsive behavior and intense relationships.**

My Second House

Once again, I made a financial plan on how to swing the purchase of a duplex townhouse in north Kirkland, Washington. I sold the house in West Seattle and the little equity I had earned plus another "loan" from my parents, I closed the deal on the townhouse. It was a beautiful townhouse that a single woman had owned and even had a hot tub on the patio deck. That hot tub became a magnet for my brother Jeff and his friends to spend the evenings after school while keeping an eye on Craig until it was his bed time. I was working long hours and off-shifts. I liked my duplex neighbor initially until I had some trouble with her regarding parking, noise, upkeep, etc. and she finally sold her unit. Good riddance, I thought.

I was doing surprisingly well in my registered nurse training at Everett Community College. I guess I was really motivated to make a better life for Craig and me.

In March 1990, at a Candle-Lighting Ceremony provided by the Everett Community College Nursing Department, I was one of the twenty-four graduates. My father's parents, his brother and family and his sister and husband were all there to see me graduate and go out to a celebratory dinner. I gave a heartfelt speech thanking my mother as being the sole reason for my accomplishment. If it were not for all that she did for me, I would have not been able to become a registered nurse. The supervising nurse gave each graduate a small potted Lucky Green Shamrock plant (Oxalis Regnelli) with their diploma as a symbolic gesture for the future. When I looked at all the assembled family, my father was not with them. That was probably why I gave him no credit for my success. My father was flying back from San Francisco and I would find out later that he had driven directly from SeaTac airport and was standing in the back of the room. If you looked at the group pictures of the family around me, my father was visibly leaning away. I think he was slighted, but it was my night. As far as the Lucky Green Shamrock, I had trouble remembering to water it and eventually gave it to my parents. They kept it alive to this day.

My Second Marriage

Not long after I moved to the townhouse, I met my second husband-to-be at a Kirkland bar. He was a cook/bartender and we were in love. I don't remember the specific reason, but the rocky relationship with my mother was at an all-time high. She was still watching Craig, but we were barely speaking. Don and I got married and the reception was held at Don's parent's house in North Bend, Washington, on Halloween Day, October 31, 1997. The announcement flyer read "Welcome to a Celebration!! Come join in the union of a family - Kathryn Yoko and Craig will join Donald Roy Williams as a family". Because of the friction going on between my mother and I, I did not invite my parents to the wedding or reception. I learned later that Craig had sent a flyer to them, but my mother was not going to attend. They did come to the reception to give Craig a wedding present of a new TV because his had recently quit working. I did not go to the door or see my parents.

We were all having fun in our Halloween costumes anyway.

I felt like the Williams were the family I never had, and I think that they were the best thing that had happened to me. I told my mother the same thing because I never felt like I fit in from the earliest times that I can remember. Chuck was the favorite, Jimmy became my mother's husband, and Jeff was the new baby in the family. Where did I fit in? I didn't feel like I fit in anywhere in this family unit. Clearly, my mother felt bad to hear that from me, but she and I have had a tough time being a picture-perfect mother and daughter. But now, I had found the Williams family and they truly loved and cherished me. I was good looking, I had a good profession, and I would have their grandchildren. They said that I was the best thing that happened to Don. **Intense relationship.**

My Third House

I decided that I wanted to earn the qualifications for an Emergency Room nurse. There was something inside of me that yearned for the urgency of triage, stress, high action, and limited bedside manner relationships. I was always very good at short term nursing care and patient relationships, particularly with the elderly. Perhaps my inability to make friends was facilitated by my ability to maintain distance and emotional separation from patients. So, in the Fall of 1997, I enrolled into Lewis-Clark State College, in Lewiston, Idaho.

My parents rented a truck to move us to Lewiston, Idaho. Along the way, Don was driving the VW bug and he did not get gas at the half way point, Vantage, Washington, like me and my parents. As a result, Don ran out of gas and my parents had to backtrack with a can of gas. It made the trip longer for my parents. I had a new Mustang and I raced ahead and did not know anything was wrong. I just laughed at the story when they all finally got to Lewiston, Idaho.

We rented a house in Lewiston. I traded in the Mustang at a Ford dealership and got a new gold colored Ford Fusion. It was at this house that I had my new Ford Fusion re-possessed from the driveway. I knew it was coming, but our finances were tight because I was going to school and not working as much. I just decided that we could not make the payments. Bummer, I didn't even get to remove my personal belongings from of the car. **Emotional swings.**

I sent this Christmas card to my parents. The card showed a cartoon of a reindeer passing gas and the card read:

> Do you hear what I hear?
>
> I wrote: *"Thanks so much for helping me move to Lewiston, and thanks for always being there for me. I don't say it enough, but I love you very much. Hope to see ya over the Holiday. Love Kathy and Craig   PS: It's snowing here!"*

Once again, driving around the area, I found a house for sale in Uniontown, Washington. It was an early American 1900's house that needed some repair but had decorative shingle siding that was colorful and freshly painted. It was a rent to buy opportunity, so we jumped on it. The house had code violations, so the owner was open to any option to get out from under it. Once again, I had a financial plan on getting this house. I was pretty good at decorating and the house looked very homey. We settled into our new home in Uniontown. Life was not without problems. We had chickens and a rooster that "cock-a-doodle do" every morning at first light. One neighbor complained that we were in violation of city code for having chickens in town. Of course, I fought it all the way to city hall and lost. We had to pay a fine and get rid of the chickens. Never talked to that neighbor again. **Emotional swings.**

The restaurant that Don was working at was going up for sale. Everybody knew that food service was a tough business. I asked my grandmother in Spokane, Washington for a loan of $20,000. Her husband, my grandfather, had recently passed away and I knew that my grandfather would not have been willing to lend me the money. Borrowing money was a sensitive issue in my mother's family. The only time my mother borrowed money from her father was when she needed money to file for divorce from Ted Smith and she paid it back as quick as she could. Obviously upset, my grandmother called my mother to ask her what she should do. My mother was extremely upset that I would prey on a vulnerable old lady who lost her husband. My mother felt that with my re-payment history, the loan would be gone as soon as the restaurant folded. As a result, my mother and I were not talking again. **Emotional swings, emptiness, and dissociative symptoms.**

On July 29, 1997, I sent this letter to my mother:

> *"Mom – Add this to my 'fucked up daughter" tab and send me the bill. Craig won't be coming* (he was scheduled to visit) *Don't worry. This is not your poor victimized daughter talking...you never believed me anyway. I have a new life, a new family, (that will actually <u>invite me</u> on vacation). So good ridding. I hope you and Uncle Lonnie choke on every dime of Grandpa's money. Enjoy!! Kathy PS I will never forgive you for making me look like a criminal to Grandma. Shame on you!!"* **Abandonment, intense relationships, emotional swings, emptiness, and dissociative symptoms.**

Life's Challenges

A good thing happened and that was my daughter, Melissa was born on September 22, 1999.

Craig was almost a teenager and getting interested cars. I decided to give Craig an incentive to do good in school and stay away from drugs. I told him that he could have my yellow 1973 Volkswagen Super Beetle when he turned 15. Uniontown, Washington was in farm country and you could get a driver's license at age 15. Craig was in heaven with the thought of having a car. He started saving his money and putting it into the car. He got it painted, bought new tires and a stereo system. It was parked in the garage next to the house but there was no lock on the garage door. One night, someone stole the stereo and slashed the tires. I think it was a couple of brothers that Craig had be-friended at school. It was my feeling that they were jealous of Craig's material wealth. The rest of the VW bug story was that my parents came and towed it back to Redmond, Washington so no further damage could be done to it. Before Craig turned age 16, I sold the car and kept all the money. I was hurting for money and Craig was being a butt.

In July 2000, my parents rented a large house at Lake Chelan, Washington, and invited us to spend a week with the family. Jimmy's mom, Jimmy's brother and his two kids, Chuck and his kids, and my brother Jeff were all vacationing in this waterfront home. One afternoon, Jimmy's brother, Chuck, Don, Jeff and I went out drinking in the town of Chelan, Washington. Jeff got bombed and attempted to disrupt the band. Chuck grabbed Jeff's arm to stop him and he stumbled and hit his head on a table's edge. Bleeding profusely, we left the bar and headed to the hospital. I applied pressure to the cut and Jeff was asking if he was going to die. Jeff got stitches to his head and was belligerent to the hospital staff. Later as he sobered up, he was very remorseful for his actions. When I told my parents what had happened, I kind of laughed as I told them that Jeff thought he was going to die. My parents were very upset that someone didn't stop the drinking and return home. This was a family vacation and not the time for heavy drinking and being drunk around the children. To top it off, Don and I smoked a joint in our bedroom and my mother smelled the odor and was pissed. I just laughed as we prepared to leave the next day. **Impulsive behavior**.

On October 7, 2000, Jeff died unexpectedly of Hypertrophic Cardio Myopathy while on the way to a surfing trip on the Oregon coast. Jeff and his friends had played basketball, had a couple of beers at a pub and Jeff went to sleep on the couch of his friend's apartment in Olympia, Washington. Jeff never woke up and his friends tried to revive him, but to no avail. Medic I arrived and thought it was just a drug overdose. My parents were devastated, and family and friends were steadily streaming to their house to comfort them and express their sympathy. I came to the house and was grieving in my own way. I decided to drive to the ocean, leaving Melissa at my parent's house. I knew my mom was continually crying and mostly lying in the bedroom, but I knew she would take care of Melissa while I was gone. Besides, there were many people in the house to keep an eye on her. I was seven months pregnant and I just wanted to get away from all the grief and to be on my own. After some eight or nine hours, my mom called Don to come and get Melissa. I guess babysitting was not therapeutic to my mom's grieving process. She was mad that I would leave Melissa with all that was going on at the house. They were busy acknowledging the sympathies of visiting friends, answering telephone calls, and entertaining guests, so to speak. My parents and all those present were in stunned disbelief that Jeff was gone. I did what I had to do as we all grieve differently. **Extreme emotional swings.**

A Christmas to Remember

On December 16, 2000, I gave birth to a baby boy who I named Cory. I wanted to name him for my mother's maiden name and my younger brother who passed away just two months prior but Cory it was. While in the hospital, Don accidently dropped Cory on his head next to the bed. I went ballistic. Probably, my emotional state was affected by post-partum. At any rate, I screamed at Don asking how he could be so careless and stupid. The hospital staff immediately went into action by examining Cory and administering a CT scan. Luckily, all tests were normal, and no injury was detected. I know Don felt terrible and he realized that I did not mean all that I had said to him. I was on pain pills for a Caesarean section delivery that contributed to my state of mind. **Intense relationships, unstable emotions or moods and intense anger.**

Because I had been on maternity leave, we had been going to the food bank as finances were tight without me working. Don was working part time as a cook at a nearby diner. Someone nominated me to receive a Christmas gift from the community. The volunteers came to the house with a bicycle for Craig, toys for the Melissa and Cory, toiletries for Don and me, and food. What a surprise. Here we were considered a needy family when I made sixty to seventy thousand dollars a year working as a nurse. We were still always living from paycheck to paycheck because the more I made, the more I spent. I defined "instant gratification" before that term became popular with the tech boom aged crowd. **Unstable self-image, impulsive behavior and emotional swings.**

I decided to invite my parents to spend Christmas with our new family in Uniontown, Washington. There was snow on the ground and it felt like Christmas. Don and Craig helped to get the house cleaned and ready for company. The house looked homey and was cleaner than it ever had been. It looked like a country farm house in a magazine. I always had a touch for arranging furniture and decorative items. There were homemade quilts on the beds. I even cooked a turkey with all the trimmings for Christmas dinner.

During the visit, we went to Craig's Christmas play and watched him play in a basketball game for Colton High. My father commented that Craig was playing position defense just as the coach had taught him. He was very disciplined in maintaining position and rotation. Craig did not have the same physical athleticism of kids who have been playing basketball since they were five years old. This was the best visit that I had ever had with my parents. Everything was perfect, and everybody was on their best behavior. My father told me that this was the best Christmas that he could remember ever having with me and my family. Maybe my post-partum condition over-powered what would be later identified as

Borderline Personality Disorder and made me more "normal". My parents said they had a very nice and memorable Christmas dinner and stay.

Good Times Don't Last Forever

In April 2001, I sent a card with an Asian kid as Elvis on the cover and the card read:

> Thankyouverymuch!
>
> I wrote: *"Dear Jimmy (and mom), Just wanted to say 'thanks' for getting the Bug – I know it wasn't cheap to do that, not to mention all the time...Thanks a million – I really do appreciate it!! Love Kathy XXXOOOXXX*

There had been good and bad times, but life continued to move on. My marriage was beginning to sour. I found myself on the internet seeking love through on-line dating. Longing to take advantage of the additional Emergency Room nurse training, I decided it was time to move back to the Seattle area. We terminated the agreement to buy the house in Uniontown, and moved into Don's parent's house in North Bend, Washington. I found a job as an Emergency Room nurse and was making good money. Don was waiting for a job at the new casino coming to town. My relationship with Don had deteriorated to the point that I eventually left with the kids. I got into a big argument with Don's mother, and we lashed out hurtful things at each other. I changed my tone on the Williams being the family I never had. Don's mother was very bitter and verbally negative about me and openly voiced her feelings to my parents. **Unstable relationships, impulsive behavior, and explosive anger.**

Going to Shelton and Starting New

Looking for something different, I took a nursing position at a hospital in Shelton, Washington. I found a great house to rent with the option to buy. On-line dating connected me up with a German man in the historic town of Dresden, Germany. I sent some money and his grandmother funded a trip to Seattle. Dieter graduated as a mechanical engineer but had not been able to find a job in his field. Dieter was an only child and his parents were worried about their son going to America. Dieter was a nice guy and was good with the kids. He could not work in America until he got a green card. His English was good, but he was a little hard to understand with his accent. **Intense relationships.**

In December 2001, I invited my parents to Shelton, Washington, for Cory's birthday party. Don and his girlfriend were at the party, and it was the first time my parents met Dieter. It was awkward as Don and I were still legally married, but everyone behaved and were there for Cory's birthday party. I gave Cory a bottle of Mike's Hard Lemonade and he guzzled it like a baby's bottle of milk. I thought it was funny and saw nothing wrong with it. Cory really liked alcohol. My parents were aghast at what had just happened, and my mother said, "why do you think this was funny? Giving alcohol to a baby was illegal and given your family history of alcohol abuse, it was just insane." That was all my parents could take and they left. ***Impulsive behavior and dissociative symptoms.***

On May 28, 2002 at 9:12 AM, I sent this email to my mother:

> ***Subject: Hi Mom. What to say. I have to write this e-mail, because if I told you my feelings over the phone, even the slightest disappointment in your voice would literally be the end of me. Every day, I think God made a mistake. He didn't mean to take Jeff, he was supposed to***

take me. Why would he take someone that you so young and full of life, the very epitome of a "Good Son" and leave someone behind so miserable, in pain, and a chronic disappointment to her parents. Like you, I think I've decided to hate God. I know by saying that you probably feel this is just another one of your daughter's pathetic ways of trying to get attention. I have to accept that you probably feel this way. For whatever reason, we have never been as close as I wish we could be, this coupled with the depression and medical problems, it just seemed the easy way out to go live with Jeff. I just wanted to stop hurting. For whatever reason, I have to accept that I need to stay right now. Sometimes I think my life is just a cruel joke by God. In saying this, the sum of this enlightenment has forced me to take a leave of absence from my responsibilities. I am so sick right now that I'm a terrible mother, wife and nurse. It is a struggle to get out of bed each day, now it's got to a point I can't even eat. I told the counselor, "I can't afford to take a leave of absence from my life". He simply said, "You can't afford not too". It is clear my only trust I have left in the medical community is in Bette Tong so would appreciate if you could coordinate a visit with her, either June 6th or after the 8th. I just can't do anything for myself right now. I just have to focus on getting my feet on the floor each day and take a day at a time. I love you Mom. Kathy

Intense fear of abandonment, distorted self-image, suicidal behaviors, extreme emotional swings, feelings of emptiness, and severe dissociative symptoms.

On February 6, 2003 at 4:00 AM, I sent this email to my mother:

Subject: Helloooooooo, You must be about done with your afternoon meal. I still feel the rhythm of your life, even when I am not there. I love you so much. Today is filled with "run around" again. Craig has his meeting with the drug and alcohol counselor at 9:30, and that will take 2 hours. The weather has been cold, but beautiful outside. I plan on taking the children to the park during this time. Perhaps you have seen a picture of this park, on the Shelton website?? It is a large play structure, built of wood, looking like a fortress. Stay busy today my baby, and I am saying sorry now, that again, your mailbox will be empty, for the next several hours. I know I have many questions to answer, from the last few e-mails you have sent, and I promise to answer them soon. By the way, palmade is a type of cream that you put in your hair, to make it look shiny. What day did you send Craig's CD's?? I am curious as to what day I should

> expect it. You will find a Valentine's box, arriving at your house too, before February 14th. It has taken me so long, to get it "together". So, my Dieter, I will close for now, in hopes that maybe I can sleep 2 more hours. Melissa actually slept in her own bed last night. I love you Very, Very Much!!! Don't Ever Doubt That!! Work Hard My Baby, and you TOO, keep your ears stiff! In deepest love, Kathy XXXOOOXXX"

This was a strange message that was intended for Dieter but sent to my mother. Based on the early morning hour of the writing perhaps it was just a mistake, but it occurred during a time of increasing confusion and strange thinking.

April 6, 2003 I sent an e-mail card and wrote:

> Dear Mom, Mom, you're always doing a million things…& what does it get U? Now you are

finally 60. It seems like such a huge milestone. I thank you for all the things you do for me. They seem like such trite words, but I really do mean it. If I don't tell you enough, know that I Love You...Also know, that I am Thankful that you are my mother. You have such a huge influence as to WHO I am today. I Thank You for always teaching me to be strong and independent, and though not perfect, always encouraging me to be my best. I Hope The Next 20 Years Will Bring Us Closer, I really do care for you. Have a Wonderful Birthday!! I Hope You can get together with some of the kids and have a good day!! Love, Kathy

Craig has a girl friend named Amanda whose home life was a bit shaky. I felt sorry for her and let her move in with us. Although, she was helpful with the babysitting, it was like having another teenage in the family. Amanda was into drugs and Craig was getting back into drugs that he had started in Uniontown, Washington. Life in Shelton, Washington was beginning to wear thin and it was time to move again. I wanted to be closer to my mother as she was diagnosed with ovarian cancer in October 2003. Before we left Shelton, Washington, I kicked Amanda out of the house. However, I felt sorry for her and let her move to Redmond, Washington, with us.

I found an apartment on the shores of Lake Sammamish in Redmond, Washington. The apartment was expensive and too small for all of us, but we stuck it out. It was close to my parent's home, so my mom would be available to babysit in a pinch. My mother was getting a lot of cancer treatments and I was working as much as I could to pay the rent and other expenses, so we didn't see her much. **Impulsive behavior.**

On May 19, 2005 at 8:17 AM, I sent this e-mail to my mother:

> *Subject: Breaking My Heart. Dear Mom, What have I done? Why is it so easy for you to exclude me out of your life? Maybe it's because I lied about why I needed money in December? I was too ashamed to admit that I didn't have any money to buy my children Christmas presents. I'm sorry I lied. I constantly feel like I can't be truthful to you and Jimmy, because I always feel a great deal of shame that I can't make ends meet for my family. I am truly sorry. Maybe you are mad that I haven't Thanked You enough for all you did for Craig. Well I do Thank You. I Thank You very much. I bought a nice card to try and verbalize what you did for me and Craig. I didn't send it, because it was petty as my Birthday gift to you. It would mean nothing. I'm so sorry that I didn't have the money to*

show you how much I do. More than you could ever know. Maybe you are mad at me for gaining my weight back. You are too ashamed to have me seen in public with you. Or does it have something to do with something Craig said? Craig was extremely hurt by you accusing him of using meth. He tried to sting you back, by pulling something out of context that I told him months earlier. (i.e.: ovarian cancer is a painless cancer). Craig accused you of using narcotics for your hip. This was a conversation between you and Craig and I am getting blamed for this. You know mom, I have never told you that I thought you didn't love me. This is your own internal dialogue. I don't understand how you can constantly use me as the scapegoat. It hurts me so much. Of all people you should know how precious time is. As much as it hurts you to lose Jeff, I can't understand why would you force that same pain on your own child. The only thing I want from you is time. Please don't equate money for love. I need so much more. If I could (honestly) change places with Jeff, I would. I have told myself this a million times. I am so sorry that it wasn't me. It would have been so much less painful for everyone. Why did God take away Jeff instead of me? Why, why, why? Jeff had so much to live for and I am just a piece of shit. I have no value to anyone. My self-esteem is buried deep inside my Mother's heart. If my own mother can't bear the sight of me, then how can I love myself? How can anybody love me? Why should I even continue to suffer with this heartbreak? I moved my family back home to spend every precious moment with you. I moved here to search for that grace (Oprah) and peace in our relationship before you die. I am not worthy of that. As much as you give to others, you deserve much more from your daughter. I love you very much.

I'm sorry that even this has no value. My love is worthless. My heart is so heavy that I can't carry it around anymore. I feel like I have no purpose. I have nothing. My heart is crushed. I'm so sorry it wasn't me…..God made a mistake and you are suffering for it. I'm so sorry it wasn't me.

Fear of abandonment, intense relationships, distorted self-image, suicidal behaviors, emotional swings, and severe dissociative symptoms.

On September 14, 2006, I asked my parents for $1,450.00 for Bariatric Surgery. I have tried for years of dieting to lose weight with up and down success. I wanted to look good and find a man who will see me as a professional nurse and a pretty woman. My parents tried to change my mind about the surgery because of all the risks associated with it. They said that it was not an easy, risk-free operation and that it meant big changes in what and how much you chose to eat after the surgery. It was not a panacea for all overweight people. I convinced them that I was committed to a new life that included Dieter. **Feelings of emptiness.**

Living in Redmond and My Third Marriage

My relationship with my mom was still strained but I decided to move to a larger apartment near Microsoft and less than mile from my parent's house. I needed my mother to babysit the kids even though we were barely speaking to each other. I was worried about Cory because he seemed to be progressing at a slower rate than normal babies and he seemed to be sick often. I started taking him to different doctors because he had many, different symptoms. Being a nurse, I felt like I knew more than the doctors sometimes. I kept describing symptoms and seeking a diagnosis. My mother was beginning to think that I had Munchausen Syndrome by Proxy (MSBP) because there was a big case back East on TV and many news articles about it lately. The story of a mother intentional harming her child seemed so bazaar and it was getting a lot of news coverage. I was surprised that my mother would think that I was making up or causing illness or injury to Cory. In the end, there was something up with Cory and my insistence upon the doctors to figure out what was wrong, finally led to a diagnosis of Asperger Syndrome. I was relieved that a diagnosis was finally determined, and early aggressive intervention and treatment would be very beneficial. **Unstable emotions and dissociative symptoms.**

Dieter and I went on a vacation to Dresden, Germany to meet his parents and grandmother. They were nice to me, but I felt the concern that they had that I was not the type of woman they were hoping for their son. We had a good time and I met many of Dieter's friends. Most of them spoke only German so I was not clear as to how they felt about me. Dieter showed me all the sights around this historic town that was devastated by World War II and restored to its original grandeur. **Distorted self-image and dissociative symptoms.**

I divorced Don and got into a legal battle for the custody of the kids. Don claimed that I was a prescription drug addict and alcoholic and unfit to have the kids. I hired a lawyer and won joint custody. My mother submitted a letter to the court stating her experiences with Don's claim of being the full- time custodian of the kids during our marriage. After resolving those legal issues, Dieter and I got married at City Hall in Seattle, Washington. My mother and a family woman friend were there to witness the marriage. **Intense relationships, emotional swings, intense anger and paranoia.**

Meanwhile, Craig and Amanda were driving me nuts. They ate all the food and they made a mess all around the apartment. I got on them all the time to pick up after themselves. Finally, I kicked Craig out of the apartment prior to his senior year and he moved into my parent's house. Amanda went back home to her family in Shelton, Washington, but managed to get back up to see Craig every weekend. Craig was not liking Redmond

High School and made a commitment to Best Alternative High School in Kirkland, Washington for his senior year and graduated. My father helped Craig with his senior project that was a requirement for graduation. My parents gave Craig a graduation present of a Toyota pick-up truck that belonged to Jeff. ***Intense relationships, emotional swings, and intense anger.***

Dieter and I were starting to have marital problems. I think he was seeking out other women and he was drinking heavily. He got a DUI and was no longer driving. I was working a lot and he was on the computer all the time. He was working and had begun an apprenticeship program to be a butcher. One day, we had a big fight with shoving and pushing. I called the police in a hysterical state and they took my statement that Dieter had beaten me up. Dieter had gone to my parent's house to avoid the police and my parents convinced him to go back to the apartment. The police questioned Dieter separately and he showed them the scratch marks he had on his body. I was crying and yelling, and the police ended up arresting me and I spent a couple of days in jail because it was the weekend and a court appointed lawyer was not available until Monday. Finally, on Tuesday morning I was released, and a court hearing date was scheduled. I guess the police found Dieter more creditable because he was calm and sounded reasonable. I was hysterical and out of control, so the police decided that I was the problem. That's the story of my life. **Intense relationships, unstable self-image, extreme emotional swings and explosive anger.**

Craig and Amanda moved into Sixty O One apartments in Redmond, Washington. It was ironic that this was the same apartment complex that my mother's cheating boyfriend, Gil Stratford, had lived while dating my mother. Craig and Amanda were both working but eventually they separated. Craig told me that Amanda's drug addiction was too much for him to deal with.

Earlier, I mentioned that the Williams family took me and the kids on vacation, well truth be told, my parents took me and my family on many vacations. One that comes to mind was when my parent drove their motorhome to Lake Goodwin near Stanwood, Washington and rented a cabin for Melissa, Cory and me. It was summertime and very warm and we were right on the lake shoreline. My brother Chuck and his youngest daughter were tenting next to the motorhome. Chuck and I were getting along marginally. My relationship with my mother was strained but we were trying to make a go of it. Melissa and Cory would not leave the motorhome, in spite of the beautiful weather and swimming in the lake just a few feet away. My parents were upset that they couldn't get the kids to go outside and play. Instead, they insisted on making a mess in the motorhome. One could cut the tension in the air with a blunt knife. Finally, my mother told the kids to go outside and play. I got so mad and very upset. I decided to leave after only one day of the weeklong vacation. I wrote this note to my parents and packed up and drove away without saying a word. **Unstable self-image and unstable emotions or moods**

> ***Mom & Dad, Thanks so much for inviting us camping. I don't think anyone of us could have predicted how stressful this would turn out to be. All those years I wanted so bad to be included in family events and now that I was, I realize why I was never invited. So, so, so sorry for ruining your trip. I know you paid a lot of money for the cabin for it all to turn out like this. Thanks Again – And Sorry Kathy***
>
> ***Feelings of emptiness***

My Mother Abandons Me

My mother had been experiencing stomach problems, hip pain and back issues when in October 2003, she was diagnosed with Stage 4 Ovarian Cancer. She had two surgeries, many Chemo therapy sessions, experimental drug treatments, but there was no hope. Part of the cancer treatment included sessions with a psychiatrist to understand the stressful relationship between my mother and me. Information from these sessions led to a diagnosis of Borderline Personality Disorder to explain my behavior. She died on April 1, 2007. I hated her, but she was the only one that cared for me. **Abandonment and feelings of emptiness**

In the years just prior to my mother's death, I was struggling with life. Now my third marriage was on the rocks. My relationship with my oldest son, Craig was good and bad but mostly bad. My youngest son, Cory was trying to overcome the symptoms of Asperger

Syndrome. My health had not been good, and I had been hospitalized a several occasions for kidney stones, a bowel obstruction, alcohol poisoning, infections, gall bladder surgery, etc. I needed my mother's help with babysitting, driving the kids and helping me deal with my health issues even though she was suffering the side effects of cancer treatment. During this time, my mother and I were still at odds because of all the situations that had occurred in recent years. I didn't spend much time with my mother as she got worse and worse and closer to death. I was good at nursing duties that she might need but was little comfort to her. I got into an argument with my father and the hospice nurse over the decision to move her to Evergreen Hospice, in Kirkland, Washington. I knew that my mother wanted to die at home, but my father, and the nurse agreed, that the time had come to move her to Hospice because the level of care had gotten too difficult. My father told me that he would hear me out, but in the end that the decision was his to make. **Emotional swings**

Added to all the stress in my life, my mother was approaching the final stages of life. I would soon be **abandoned** by my mother. On the third evening that she was in Hospice, I called ahead to ask the nurse to have all other family and relatives removed from the room, so I could have a private hour with my mother. My father said he was surprised that I just did not ask because everyone present would have easily accommodated my request. I did not want to talk with anyone and, didn't before or after my private hour with my mother. I made my peace with her even though she was unconscious. I think the nurse understood my request, as us nurses need to stick together, but she must have sensed my animosity toward my family. **Emotional swings, feelings of emptiness, and inappropriate anger.**

At my mother's funeral, my kids and I chose not to sit with the family in the first two rows. I can't say that my father was overly welcoming in trying to get us to sit with the family. I don't remember talking with any of the family and friends that were gathered at the reception following the service. I was lost, and the sad fact was that the one person I leaned on the most was now gone. **Abandonment, emotional swings, and feelings of emptiness.**

After a couple of weeks, my father asked me if I wanted some of my mother's belongings. I took bags and bags of her nicer clothing and took them to a consignment store. I took all her gold jewelry. I asked about her pain medications which included Oxycontin, Oxycodone and Fentanyl. I kiddingly asked my father if I could have them and he said he would took care of disposing the drugs. My father signed over the title to my mother's fairly, new, Subaru Outback. He had new brakes and maintenance service done on the car. The timing was perfect because my Ford Explorer was on its last legs. Shortly after getting the Subaru, I put a dent on the fender in a parking garage and decided to sell it to a dealership in exchange for a Chrysler PT Cruiser and a Honda Prelude for Craig. I guess I just couldn't drive my mother's car as it was a constant reminder of her and what she must be thinking about me. ***Emotional swings, feelings of emptiness, and dissociative symptoms.***

I have always been a big spender rather than a saver, thus always had money problems. I was materialistic and always wanted to have items or give the latest in fad gifts to my children. I would say that unless I was sick or disabled, I was able to find work. Finding work meant I had money to spend. As it turned out, nursing was an excellent field for full employment whether it was at nursing home, hospital, doctor office, clinic, urgent care facility, hospice, prison, skilled nursing facility, personal care, rehab clinic, or on call as a temporary help nurse.

Here is a list of the places that I have work:

1978-1981 – Certified Nursing Assistant – Cascade Vista Convalescent Center, Redmond, WA

1981-1982 – Ward Aide – Virginia Mason Medical Center, Seattle, WA

1986-1989 - Medical Assistant – CHEC Medical Centers, Seattle/Eastside, WA

1989 - Camp Nurse/GPN – Hidden Valley, Granite Falls, WA

1989-1990 - LPN/Medical Assistant- Evergreen Urgent   Care Center, Woodinville, WA

1990-1991 - Register Nurse – Providence Hospital, Everett, WA

1991-1996 – Emergency Charge Nurse – Group Health Hospital, Seattle, WA

1997-1998 - Emergency Department Supervisor, Tri-State Memorial Hospital, Clarkston, WA

1998-2002 - House Supervisor/Nurse, Pullman Memorial Hospital, Pullman, WA

2002-2004 – House Supervisor, Mason General Hospital, Shelton, WA

2002-2007 – Emergency Department Agency RN, Star-Med Staffing Solution, Renton, WA

2007-2009 - Emergency Department Charge Nurse, Swedish Medical Center, Seattle, WA

I found that working as an Emergency Room Agency RN was the best for me from 2009 until 2012. The pay was good, the hours flexible and the shift arrangements favorable. I made good money in the Emergency Room, but the stress was beginning to be a problem for my mental health. I had worked at all the major hospitals in the Seattle area. Unfortunately, I may not have left each job under the best of circumstances. You could say I had burnt some bridges behind me and the prospects of long term employment, outside of the Emergency Room, with a major hospital in the Seattle area were slim.

A newspaper article published in the Seattle Times on December 22, 2013, and written by Aaron Gouveia, Salary.com, listed the nine most stressful occupations. The nine most stressful jobs were Teacher, Social Worker, Newspaper Reporter, Emergency Dispatcher, ER Registered Nurse, Police Officer, Firefighter, Surgeon and Enlisted Military Personnel. Interestingly, ER Registered Nurse was second to Surgeon in annual median salary. No question it was a stressful job.

Insights into My Mind Through Greeting Cards

I think it was helpful to understand that I really tried to be a good daughter by sending cards for various occasions. I don't remember the dates of these greeting cards that I sent but the important thing was the messages they contained, both the greeting card message and my words.

> **A hand-colored card with the words written:** *"To the Dearest Mom on Mother's Day. I love you. I think you are the world. I love you. Kathy***

> **A card read: For Mom and Dad – A special wish – At this season of beginnings when the world seems bright and new. There's no end to all the happiness that's being wished for you! Happy Easter, Happy Spring.**
> **I wrote:** *"Mom and Jimmy – I can't thank you enough – Love Kathy XXXOOO"*

> A card read: From your daughter on Mother's Day – mom, you'll always be my best friend – Happy Mother's Day.
> I wrote *"Words can't express how much you mean to me. Thanks for being my mom! Love, Kathy XXXOOOXXX"*

> A card read: Mom, we thought we'd tidy up the house for you on Mother's Day! We're going to put Dad in the yard.
> I wrote: *"Mom – Happy Mom's Day. Thanks for everything you do! Love, Kathy XXXOOOXXX"*

> A card read: Happy Birthday to a dad who went through Hell raising a devil like me!
> I wrote: "Jimmy, Have a Happy Birthday always. Love Kathy"

A card read: For a special mom and dad...special for your warmth and understanding...for your love and your caring...for just being the wonderful parents you are!

I wrote: *"Mom and Dad – Merry Christmas with Love Merry Christmas – Love from your daughter, Kathy XXXOOOXXX"*

A card read: 'Tis the season to be Ollie...Happy Holidays (Do not shred until after December 25) Oliver North's picture was on the cover.

I *wrote "Mom – saw this card and thought of you. Love, Kathy"*

A card read: Wishing you the gentle joys of peace and love this holiday season. Merry Christmas.

I wrote: *"Dear Mom, Jimmy and Jeff, Wishing you a happy holiday season. Love, Kathy and Craig"*

> A card read: I love you, Mom! More than words can say, more than hugs can show. Mom, I love you lots – more than you could know! Happy Mother's Day.
> I wrote: *"Mom – Love, Kathy & Craig XXXOOOXXX"*

These greeting cards and messages indicated, for the most part, warm and sincere messages of love and caring. There was a little sarcasm but nothing that would be atypical for a young person's thinking of their parents. The curious element was the emotional swings from Love to Hate when comparing these cards with the events occurring with my parents. Sometimes, these swings changed rapidly in both directions. ***Intense relationships and emotional swings.***

Life Alone and No Good Luck

I found a nice apartment across the boulevard from Lake Washington. There was a park at the waterfront that was perfect for the kids to play. Dieter was a frequent visitor and was living there part-time. This was a nice residential area and I was paying about $1,500 per month. Melissa and Cory were going to the same grade school, Lakeview Elementary in Kirkland, Washington, that Chuck and I attended. I was working as an agency nurse, so the pay was good, and the schedules were favorable to single parenting. I was doing some online dating to fill my time but saw no serious relationships developing. My good luck with this apartment changed when the owners of the complex did some upgrading to the units and raised the rent significantly.

One night, I had been drinking heavily and I suddenly had a terrible pain in my stomach/pancreas area. Dieter was at work, so I somehow got up and made it to my car.

God must have been watching over me as I somehow drove myself to the front of the Emergency Entrance at Overlake Hospital in Bellevue, Washington. I stumbled into the Emergency Room and was immediately hospitalized. The next day, I called my father because Hospital security told me I needed to move my car from the patient loading zone. My father moved the car into the hospital garage and I met his new wife for the first time. I looked like a pathetic mess, but I could not help it. The meeting was brief, and I was in no position to have done anything different. **Abandonment and emotional swings.**

On May 6, 2008, I was late picking up the kids from daycare. It was 4:50 PM and I was late. My father had picked up the kids. I was having a tough day and my father thought that I looked like I was drunk or drugged. Maybe I was because life was a bitch. **Self-destructive behavior.**

On March 13, 2009, I write this letter to my father:

"Dear Dad, Thanks so much for all the help you have given to me. I know that medication ended up to lots of money, and I want you to know I really appreciated it. This is a 21-day program at Sundown M Ranch for alcohol treatment. But I was given the 'gift', which means I was extended another 7 days. I will come home for less than 2 weeks to 'get some shit done', and return to Yakima for another 90 days for intensive outpatient treatment. Outpatient treatment is mandatory – Thursday, 6pm – 9 pm. I will be moving into a clean and sober house during that time. It has a lot of rules to live there, but that's what I need. My lease is up at the end of this month at the apartment, so Dieter and I are going to lease a more affordable one-bedroom apartment there instead. The kids have been moved to the

Snoqualmie School District instead. I haven't seen them for a month, and I miss them so bad. Part of AA's program is to make amends to all I have hurt. I have hurt you a lot over the years financially ($) and I hope I can right that wrong in the recovery process. Craig and Dieter just left yesterday after a 3-day family program at the ranch. It helped the family a lot to see how alcoholism is a disease – one that I will always have, but treated right, I can put it in remission (just like cancer). I know intelligently you might understand this – because you are what we call a 'normie' can have just one drink and put it down. Alcoholics cannot. The disease just progresses and progresses and progresses. I have three options. I can get sober, be institutionalized, or die. For now, I choose to be sober. One day at a time. Love, Kathy"

Abandonment, unstable self-image, emotional swings and feelings of emptiness.

This one-bedroom apartment that I moved into to reduce the rent, was just too small especially when the kids visited for a weekend. It was time to move again. I found another apartment about 4 blocks east of downtown Kirkland, Washington. It was a nice area and the apartment was a condo that was being rented. My father helped us move in again. Seems like my parents have helped me move so many times. Dieter was there some of the time because he had no place to live. With his DUI, the treatment program, court costs, and the high cost of insurance, he relied on the bus to get around. He was doing okay but I felt sorry for him and caved in when he needed help. I still liked him, and he was good with the kids.

Life was beginning to have more downs than good times. My PT Cruiser had expired tabs and got banged up in an accident that was not my fault. The accident occurred on a street in Kirkland, Washington that was under some road construction. The other driver was a well-dressed real estate company owner who tried to pass while going in the opposite direction and ran into the side of my car. He was very apologetic and stated that his insurance would take care of the damage. We exchanged information and a couple weeks later when I didn't hear from him, I contacted the number he had given me. He denied that he was at fault and claimed that it was my fault. His lawyer contacted me and said that the matter will be decided by the court. I think when he found out what my situation was, he decided that he would take me to court knowing that I didn't have the resources to fight him. Nothing came of it and my car was damaged without repair. **Dissociative symptoms.**

It was now the Fourth of July 2012, and I was still in bed. This was a symbolic day for a declaration of independence. My independence. It seemed like it was getting harder and harder for me to get out of bed on my days off. I was sober and had been for some time. I recently got a two-year token from AA marking the anniversary. I felt so alone, and I missed my mother. The kids were living with Don and it has been a few weeks since I have seen them. I even missed Dieter but I was sure that he was getting tired of not knowing what kind of mood I was in. I was depressed and feeling sad.

My life seemed to be moving with no future ahead. I decided to take all my medication at once. I knew what this could do but in my current state of mind who cared. This was my Fourth of July celebration. I sent Craig a text message of what I had done. I felt everyone would be better off without me in their lives. On my Death Certificate it read "immediate cause of death as acute combined quetiapine, trazodone and venlafaxine intoxication – interval between onset and death is minutes". **Abandonment, intense relationships,**

impulsive and self-destructive behavior, suicidal behavior, despondency, feeling of emptiness, and severe dissociative symptoms.

There are differing opinions on the effectiveness of drugs in treating BPD. Different drugs address specific troubling symptoms experienced by an individual but was the combination of drugs that were listed on the Death Certificate a helpful prescription for treating BPD? It is relevant to examine what these drugs were prescribed to treat.

Quetiapine was used to treat symptoms of schizophrenia (a mental illness that causes disturbed or unusual thinking, loss of interest in life, and strong or inappropriate emotions). They were also used to treat or prevent episodes of mania (frenzied, abnormally excited or irritated mood) or depression in patients with bipolar disorder (manic depressive disorder, a disease that causes episodes of depression, episodes of mania and other abnormal moods). It worked by changing the activity of certain natural substances in the brain.

Trazodone was used to treat depression. It was also used to treat insomnia and schizophrenia. Trazodone worked by increasing the amount of serotonin, a natural substance in the brain that helped maintain mental balance.

Venlafaxine was in clinical trials to help depression and had a positive effect on 16% of those tested.

The Pathological Diagnoses of the Autopsy Report was 1) Acute combines quetiapine, trazodone and venlafaxine intoxication. 2) Atherosclerotic cardiovascular disease with coronary artery atherosclerosis with up to 50% stenosis. 3) obesity, mild. Opinion: This 48-year old woman, who was found deceased in her residence, died of acute combined quetiapine, trazodone and venlafaxine intoxication. The manner of death was suicide. The Autopsy Report noted that there were no external or internal injuries and that all organs and systems were unremarkable except for the artery stenosis mentioned above. Also, the Toxicology Report noted that the test for the presence of amphetamines, barbiturates, benzodiazepines, cannabinoids, cocaine metabolite, methadone, opiates, phencyclidines (PCP), propoxyphene and tricyclic antidepressants resulted in none being detected.

Dieter wrote this e-mail to my father, Subject: Kathy, on July 31, 2012 at 7:37 AM:

> **Dear Jimmy, I am writing you in deepest respect and sympathy. The news about Kathy's death has shocked me as everybody else. I am glad this wonderful memorial in love and dignity was given to her. Sitting in between those people honoring Kathryn's life, I was overcome by the question: What did I really know about her?...and I concluded: not very much... Yes, I**

was exposed to her on a daily basis, I was part of this chaos that drove our life together. Resentments and anger have been exchanged very often, which turned into silence towards the end of our relationship. I simply couldn't stand this never- ending stress anymore. I was held responsible for her shortcomings and wrong decisions she made. Those circumstances made me decide moving on by June of this year. Jimmy, I have really enjoyed the very few moments which I could share together with you and Diane. I always wished we could have grown closer together as a family. Life has taken us on different paths. We only came to you in moments of despair. There was barely any time given to interact as a family. I am really sorry! I also feel I have failed making Kathryn happy. Until today, I don't know how I could have been successful... Kathryn is finally

finding peace and her soul has time to rest...
Sincerely, Dieter

The end of Kathy's story was that she had made a real start and commitment to beat alcoholism. It would continue to be a battle every day. Street drugs were not present in her system and that was a big positive. She had other demons that she would have to fight. We will never know if she would have been able to weather the challenges that she would have faced.

As you read Kathy's story you may have felt that many signs of BPD were missed. Life is an interesting journey. Everyone faces with a multitude of incidents in their lifetime filled with happiness and sadness. The hope of this book is that it helps someone to see a pattern of behavior that is worthy of seeking professional help. Borderline Personality Disorder is getting more and more attention so if any of the nine BPD symptoms are present, and certainly if five symptoms are detected, raise the white flag to get help.

Notes

Mason, M.S., Paul T and Randi Kreger, 1998. *Stop Walking on Eggshells.* Oakland, CA: New Harbinger Publications.

References

Mason, M.S., Paul T. and Randi Kreger. 1998. *Stop Walking on Eggshells,* Oakland, CA., New Harbinger Publications, Inc.

Moskovitz, M.D., Richard A. 2001 Second Edition. *Lost in the Mirror.* Lanham, MD., Taylor Trade Publishing.

Van Gelder M.F.A., Kiera. 2010. *The buddha & the borderline,* Oakland, CA., New Harbinger Publications, Inc.

Kreisman, M.D., Jerold J. and Hal Straus. 2010. *I Hate You – Don't Leave Me.* New York, NY, Penguin Group (USA) Inc.

Cauwels, Janice M. 1992. *Imbroglio.* New York, NY., W.W. Norton & Company

www.ingramcontent.com/pod-product-compliance
Lightning Source LLC
Chambersburg PA
CBHW071505040426
42444CB00008B/1507